**Praise for**
*The God I Never Knew*

.

"In an hour when spiritual hunger is increasing and practical clarity is needed to avoid the confusion to which too many are vulnerable, it is a delight to affirm the wisdom, truth, and integrity with which Robert Morris speaks, teaches, and lives. I know no leader today who exceeds the trustworthiness and genuine love for people than Robert, and you will find no better person to introduce you to friendship with the Holy Spirit of the living God."

> —JACK W. HAYFORD, founder and president of The King's
> University

"I have learned more about the Holy Spirit from Robert Morris than any other pastor. His insight into this very important topic will motivate, teach, and equip us to embrace the third person of the Trinity, as well as launch all of us into a fresh new season of worship."

> —BRADY BOYD, senior pastor of New Life Church and author
> of *Fear No Evil*

"So much controversy and confusion has surrounded the topic of the Holy Spirit. In fact, most people don't understand who He is at all. In *The God I Never Knew*, Robert Morris brilliantly clears up the misconceptions and introduces the Holy Spirit as someone you will want to be your best friend."

> —CHRIS HODGES, senior pastor of Church of the Highlands
> in Birmingham, Alabama

"*The God I Never Knew* gives life-changing insight into the mystery of the Holy Spirit. If you have questions about the Holy Spirit, Morris's book will put you at ease and lead you to know and love our comforter, helper, and friend."

> —CRAIG GROESCHEL, senior pastor of LifeChurch.tv and author
> of *Weird*

"In *The God I Never Knew,* my friend Robert Morris captures the magnificent power, friendship, and treasure that God has given us in the person of the Holy Spirit. He effectively demystifies the common misperceptions associated with this part of the Godhead and will evoke a deeper passion and love for God within every reader. No matter where you are in your walk with God, this book will intensify your relationship with Him."

—STOVALL WEEMS, lead pastor of Celebration Church
in Jacksonville, Florida, and author of *Awakening*

"Pastor Robert Morris describes the Holy Spirit in a way that doesn't make you want to run from Him or think He is somehow the unimportant, scary part of the Trinity. *The God I Never Knew* does an amazing job of not only describing who the Holy Spirit is but also making you desire more of His work in your life. This is one of the most balanced approaches to the role of the Holy Spirit that I've ever seen. You have got to read this book!"

—PERRY NOBLE, founding and senior pastor
of NewSpring Church

# The God
# I Never
# Knew

## Other Books by Robert Morris

*The Blessed Life*
*From Dream to Destiny*
*The Power of Your Words*

# ROBERT MORRIS

How Real Friendship with the Holy Spirit
Can Change Your Life

# The God
I Never
Knew

WATERBROOK
PRESS

THE GOD I NEVER KNEW
PUBLISHED BY WATERBROOK PRESS
12265 Oracle Boulevard, Suite 200
Colorado Springs, Colorado 80921

ISBN 978-0-307-72970-5
ISBN 978-0-307-72971-2 (electronic)

Copyright © 2011 by Robert Morris

Cover design by Mark D. Ford

Published in the United States by WaterBrook Multnomah, an imprint of the Crown Publishing Group, a division of Random House Inc., New York.

WATERBROOK and its deer colophon are registered trademarks of Random House Inc.

Library of Congress Cataloging-in-Publication Data
Morris, Robert (Robert Preston), 1961–
    The God I never knew : how real friendship with the Holy Spirit can change your life / Robert Morris.
        p. cm.
    ISBN 978-0-307-72970-5 — ISBN 978-0-307-72971-2 (electronic)
    1. Holy Spirit. I. Title.
    BT121.3.M67 2011
    231'.3—dc22

                                        2011014029

Printed in the United States of America
2011—First Edition

10 9 8 7 6 5 4 3 2 1

SPECIAL SALES
Most WaterBrook Multnomah books are available at special quantity discounts when purchased in bulk by corporations, organizations, and special-interest groups. Custom imprinting or excerpting can also be done to fit special needs. For information, please e-mail SpecialMarkets@WaterBrookMultnomah.com or call 1-800-603-7051.

*This book is dedicated to two of my spiritual fathers, Pastor Olen Griffing and Dr. Jack Hayford, who showed me through the Scriptures and their everyday lives that we can have a vibrant, personal relationship with the Holy Spirit, and that people who believe in the person and work of the Holy Spirit can be doctrinally sound, genuinely humble, and not weird!*

# CONTENTS

# The God I Never Knew

The knock at the door startled Irene Adkins. The seventy-nine-year-old great-grandmother wasn't expecting any visitors. A cautious peek through the peephole revealed a well-dressed silver-haired gentleman with a kind face that struck her as vaguely familiar. It was something about the eyes and nose. As she opened the door, her certainty grew—the stranger definitely reminded her of someone. But who?

It would take her a while to realize that the man's face indeed bore an uncanny resemblance to one she knew better than any other—her own. Irene's seventy-three-year-old brother, Terry, had come for a surprise visit. It was quite surprising because Irene never knew she had a brother.

Back in 1932, in the depths of the Great Depression, a desperate and confused young English couple unhitched their tattered camper trailer on the side of the road and drove away. Police later found three small, hungry children inside. Irene, at ten months of age, was the youngest. The three were placed in separate foster homes and grew up unaware of the others' existence. Meanwhile, the young couple eventually achieved some stability a few years later and had another child—their son, Terry.

When Terry was fourteen, his parents revealed their shameful secret. They told him of the desperate straits in which they'd found themselves and of the wrenching decision to abandon the trio of hungry mouths they could not feed. Shortly thereafter Terry began a lifelong quest to find his siblings, especially the sister his parents had named Irene. He searched in vain for almost sixty years. Then came a breakthrough. He learned the name of the agency that had placed Irene and her siblings in foster homes. Not long there-after came the day—April 3, 2010—when Irene Adkins discovered the won-derful brother she never knew. In the discovery the rootless orphan found a source of answers to questions she had carried around in her heart all her life.

I believe I know how Irene felt. Several decades ago, after many years of struggling to live the Christian life and even working "successfully" in full-time ministry, I finally discovered the God I never knew. And in the discov-ery I found not only the source of answers to every question I've ever had but a dear friend as well. One who has made my life richer, fuller, and more excit-ing than I ever dreamed possible.

I am referring, of course, to God—the Holy Spirit.

## AN AMAZING RELATIONSHIP

I grew up in church. However, this church was part of a denomination that avoided mentioning the Holy Spirit whenever possible. Our denominational leaders treated Him a bit like the crazy uncle who shows up at Thanksgiving once every few years and horrifies everyone with his inappropriate behavior. You can't help being related to this uncle, but you hope that if you don't men-tion his name or send him a Christmas card, he will stay away.

In fact, many years ago when I prepared to leave home to attend Bible college, my pastor had just one parting word of counsel for me. I had recently given my life to Christ, and I was burning with desire to serve Him. So I eagerly waited to hear what encouragement my pastor would deliver as I entered this season of learning and preparation for ministry.

His only advice to me was, "Watch out for people who talk about the Holy Spirit."

At the time I didn't know any better. So I simply nodded and filed his warning away in my mind. Now—after twenty-five years of discovering what a wonderful, kind, helpful, gentle, and wise person the Holy Spirit is; after developing an intimate friendship with Him that has made my life bet-ter and more fulfilling in countless ways; after watching the Holy Spirit help and bless people—I am grieved to think back on my pastor's advice. To be honest, it offends me.

Of course, most of us feel offended when someone thinks badly of a person we love and respect, especially when the opinion is based on lies or misunderstandings. I'm sure you've had the experience of hearing bad things about someone through a third party and forming a negative impression, only to meet that individual later and discover that he isn't the bad person you envisioned at all.

If you're like most people, you've probably been misinformed about the Holy Spirit to some degree. After more than twenty-five years of experience in ministry, I've seen firsthand that most Christians hold a distorted, inaccurate, or incomplete view of the third member of the Trinity. In fact, many frustrated believers are just as Irene Adkins was for most of her life—utterly unaware that a loving and amazing person desires to know them and to fill their empty lives with good things. Too many have resigned themselves to perpetual defeat in their battles with temptation or to stumbling through life, making decisions with nothing more than their own flawed reason to guide them. Others live a dull, powerless brand of Christianity, completely at odds with the picture of the vibrant, overcoming, advancing church of the book of Acts.

> The **DYNAMIC**, full life Jesus **PROMISED** to believers is a **NATURAL OUTGROWTH** of intimate friendship with God, the **HOLY SPIRIT**.

The dynamic, full life Jesus promised to believers is a natural outgrowth of intimate friendship with God, the Holy Spirit. Today I have an amazing relationship with the Holy Spirit, though that wasn't always true. By the time we're finished exploring this topic, you'll realize what an amazing relationship you can have with Him too.

# PART 1

# Who Is This Person?

2

# Helper

Like a lot of newly married couples, Debbie and I didn't have much at first. Even the possessions we could call our own were mostly hand-me-downs from our parents.

Our financial situation improved after a couple of years of marriage, and one day Debbie asked if I was okay with her buying a new comforter. Our current bedcover was so faded and threadbare that you could practically read the newspaper through it. Being a typical guy, I thought we'd buy a plain bedspread. So when we went shopping, I was shocked to learn that the comforter Debbie had in mind might require taking out a second mortgage on the house. Of course, I'm exaggerating. But the big and soft and puffy and colorful comforter we purchased was much fancier and more beautiful than I could have imagined.

Despite its cost, I was excited about our new acquisition. On the day we bought it, several times I caught myself imagining what it would feel like to slip beneath that soft comforter and be all toasty warm.

At bedtime I walked into our room and, to my horror, the beautiful new comforter was gone. With my best exasperated yet perplexed voice, I asked Debbie, "Sweetie, where's the new comforter?"

She gave me that look. You know the one—the "you can't seriously be that dense" look. The truth is, yes, we husbands really can be that dense! Realizing the level of my denseness in this moment, Debbie explained, "That new comforter isn't for use. It's for looks."

In the years since that night, we've accumulated many household items that I've discovered are for looks, not use. We have plates I'm not allowed to eat on and fancy goblets I can't drink from. We have beautiful towels that *you* can use if you stay at our house, but *I* can't. In fact, there are towels hanging in my bathroom right now that I'm not allowed to use.

In the same way, millions of Christians have been given a comforter, but they treat Him as if He's just for looks. If we think that way, we're wrong. The wonderful gift of the Holy Spirit is meant to be so much more than an ornamental feature in our lives.

### Introducing a Helper

Just who is the Holy Spirit? That's a big question—one as big as God Himself.

When you want to get to know someone new, often the first step is to be introduced by someone who already knows that person well. During His years of ministry on earth, Jesus knew the Holy Spirit better than any human ever had or has since. So perhaps the best place to learn about the Holy Spirit begins with Jesus and the words He used to introduce the Spirit to the disciples, as recorded in John 14.

It's helpful to know chapters 14–16 of John's gospel contain a record of Jesus's conversation with His disciples at the Last Supper. Jesus isn't publicly teaching a large crowd of casual followers and curious gawkers on a Galilean hillside. He's not debating the Pharisees or speaking cryptically in parables to the Sadducees. Instead, Jesus is in a small room, having dinner with His closest friends. He knows that in just twelve short hours, He will be put to death on the cross. In this unbelievably serious moment, a leader who knows He is about to be killed gives vital instructions and information to His followers.

Jesus begins with words of comfort: "Don't let your hearts be troubled. I'm going away, but I will come back" (paraphrased). Then, in John 14:16–17, Jesus gets to the core of what He wants these men to understand:

And I will pray the Father, and He will give you another Helper, that He may abide with you forever—the Spirit of truth, whom the world cannot receive, because it neither sees Him nor knows Him; but you know Him, for He dwells with you and will be in you.

Don't get hung up on the fact that Jesus says, "I will *pray* the Father." Using the word *pray* this way sounds a little odd to our modern ears. But the Greek word translated "pray" here is translated "ask" in many other parts of the New Testament. Jesus is simply saying, "I will ask the Father, and He will give you another Helper."

> The **TRUTH** of the Holy Spirit living with and in us **ASSURES US** that we **NEVER** have to feel **ALONE.**

Note the word "Helper." The person the Father will send sounds mysterious, but Jesus tells the disciples that the role and nature of this person is to "help." Jesus also assures them that the Helper won't be a complete stranger. "But you know Him," Jesus says.

How could they already know this coming helper? Jesus explains by saying, "For He dwells with you and will be in you." The verb "dwells" is in the present tense, while the phrase "will be in you" is clearly future tense. At the moment Jesus was speaking, the disciples had experienced the Helper dwelling "with" them to a certain extent. But the Helper was about to be sent in a way that would make Him not only "with" them but "in" them.

Although Jesus spoke these words to a small group of His closest friends and followers, they are also meant for us. The truth of the Holy Spirit's living with and in us assures us that we never have to feel alone.

## How the Holy Spirit Helps

What kind of "help" will the Holy Spirit provide? Jesus gives part of the answer in John 14:25–26:

> These things I have spoken to you while being present with you. But the Helper, the Holy Spirit, whom the Father will send in My name,

He will teach you all things, and bring to your remembrance all
things that I said to you.

This is the second time Jesus chooses the word "Helper" to describe the
One the Father is sending. Here Jesus lists two of the many ways this person
will be of help.

First, "He will teach you all things." What an incredible promise. There's
no subject in which God isn't an expert. He has all the answers. The second
way the Holy Spirit helps is by bringing "to your remembrance all things that
I [Jesus] said to you." This is one reason the Gospels are so detailed and in
such agreement about the words of Jesus. The Holy Spirit helped the disciples remember everything Jesus said to them.

## Jesus Must Leave

A little later in this conversation with the disciples, Jesus gives the third mention of the coming Helper being sent from the Father:

But when the Helper comes, whom I shall send to you from the
Father, the Spirit of truth who proceeds from the Father, He will
testify of Me. (John 15:26)

Notice that Jesus calls Him "the Spirit of truth." Jesus presents the Holy
Spirit to us as the ultimate answer to overcoming and undoing the work of
Satan, the great Deceiver and "the father of lies" (John 8:44, NIV). For thousands of years, since the fall of Adam and Eve, mankind had stumbled in the
darkness of the devil's lies. Then Jesus, who declared Himself to be "the way,
the *truth,* and the life" (John 14:6), announced He would soon be sending
a helper who would make it possible to live a life free from deception.

In John 16, Jesus gives the disciples His most thorough introduction to
the Holy Spirit. "So wonderful is this One who will be sent," Jesus tells them,
"that it is a much better thing for you if I go away. Because if I don't go, He
can't come!" That's how I like to paraphrase it—here's the actual translation:

Nevertheless I tell you the truth. It is to your advantage that I go
away; for if I do not go away, the Helper will not come to you; but
if I depart, I will send Him to you. (John 16:7)

The first thing that always strikes me when I read this passage is that
Jesus feels compelled to say, "Now, I'm telling you the truth here." He knows
that the next words He speaks will truly seem unbelievable to the disciples.
The disciples were grief stricken at the idea that Jesus would be going away
from them. They loved Him. They de-
pended on Him. He was their miracle-
working leader. How could it possibly
be good that He is about to leave them?
Jesus immediately explains that only if
He goes to the Father can the Helper
be sent.

> How could it **POSSIBLY**
> be **GOOD** that He is
> about to **LEAVE** them?

Jesus continues by explaining some more ways the Holy Spirit will provide help, and we'll look at those in a moment. Right now, notice John
16:12–14. There, Jesus says,

I still have many things to say to you, but you cannot bear them
now. However, when He, the Spirit of truth, has come, He will
guide you into all truth; for He will not speak on His own authority,
but whatever He hears He will speak; and He will tell you things to
come. He will glorify Me, for He will take of what is Mine and
declare it to you.

These verses contain an amazing promise. Jesus wants to tell the disciples the whole amazing story of what lies ahead, but He knows that the
truths He wants to deliver would just overwhelm and confuse them at this
moment. But He has good news for them. Who better to deliver important
truths than the Spirit of truth? "When He…has come, He will guide you
into all truth," Jesus says. "All truth." That's quite a benefit of friendship with
the Holy Spirit. No wonder Jesus refers to Him as the Helper.

But Jesus mentions yet another form of help the Spirit will provide: "He will tell you things to come." Let me put it a little differently. Jesus is saying, "The Holy Spirit will tell you the future." Would it occasionally be helpful to know what's around the corner? Have you ever been blindsided by some event and thought to yourself, *If only I'd known this was coming, I'd have been better prepared*?

> JESUS is saying, "The Holy Spirit will tell YOU the FUTURE."

One of the elders at the church I pastor is a wonderful model for allowing the Holy Spirit to show us things to come. Steve built a large and successful business in the ultracompetitive construction industry, largely by regularly getting alone with God and allowing His Spirit to direct him where his business is concerned.

In addition to having daily quiet times of Bible study, private worship, and prayer, Steve makes it a point to go away two or three times each year for several days at a time. He rents a cabin or lake house and takes little more than his Bible and a notebook. His testimony is that he invariably receives instruction from the Holy Spirit in these sessions of private communion about what lies ahead and how to lead his business accordingly. Steve can share instance after instance in which a seemingly counterintuitive instruction from the Holy Spirit resulted in a profitable breakthrough. Or in which a warning enabled him to avoid unnecessary losses or bad hiring decisions.

Yes, a key role of the Holy Spirit is to lead us supernaturally into truth and reveal what lies ahead. No wonder Jesus refers to the Holy Spirit as the Helper four times in three consecutive chapters! The promises in these passages are absolutely incredible. In each of these four instances, the Greek word translated "helper" is *parakletos*. The Greek word appears only five times in the entire New Testament, and we've just looked at four of them.*

When the typical first-century Greek speaker or writer used this word, he was talking about a person who pleads your case like a lawyer before a judge, or someone who goes before you to intercede with someone on your

---

* The fifth appearance of the word *parakletos* is in 1 John 2:1, which says, "And if anyone sins, we have an *Advocate* with the Father, Jesus Christ the righteous."

behalf. What an amazing way to think of who the Holy Spirit is and how He is our helper!

## The Bottom Line

The key message about the Holy Spirit's role is very simple: *He helps me.* He helps me know what to say when I'm speechless. He helps me know when to speak and when to keep my mouth closed.

I'm sure you can think of situations where both kinds of help would be welcome. For example, a friend shares a serious problem and you have no idea what to say that will help or encourage her. Then a thought suddenly comes to mind, you speak it aloud, and the person says, "Wow, that's exactly what I needed to hear!" That's what the Holy Spirit can do—giving you the very words you need to say.

Sometimes He tells you what *not* to say. Have you ever had that happen? Maybe you've been involved in a conversation with someone who got a little emotional. Just as you are about to throw out a really clever comeback, you have a little cautionary thought: *I shouldn't say that.*

Of course, the problem is that most of us say what we're thinking anyway. Invariably, we end up concluding, *I shouldn't have said that!* This happens a lot in marriage. Maybe you come home from work, and although you don't know it at that moment, your spouse has had a tough day. You start to say something, and the Holy Spirit nudges you and whispers, *I wouldn't go there if I were you, My friend.* Sometimes He adds, *As a matter of fact, if I were you, I'd take her out to dinner.* If you're smart, you'll listen and choose wisely in that moment. If you're not so smart—like me sometimes—you'll ignore that advice and speak your mind.

I've learned to listen to that voice. I've discovered how wonderful it is to have a helper.

You might be wondering if the Holy Spirit really speaks to us in such clear ways. The simple answer is yes. The truth is that most of us don't have any trouble believing that God speaks to us. We just get frustrated because we don't know exactly what He's saying. Almost every one of us has a desire, even a desperation, to hear with confidence the voice of God. Who wants to stumble through life without the benefit of the clear direction and inward peace that comes from hearing God's voice? The great news is that God doesn't want that for us either.

Hearing God's voice is vital to breaking out of old comfort zones and into exciting new levels of effectiveness. Hearing God and responding to Him can take us to new places of intimacy and purpose in Him.

> Hearing God's **VOICE** is vital to breaking out of old **COMFORT** zones and into exciting **NEW** levels of **EFFECTIVENESS**.

Hearing God's voice begins by recognizing which member of the Trinity is tasked with speaking to us in this season of history. It is, of course, the Holy Spirit. The Father is on His throne. Jesus has been seated at His right hand and, according to Hebrews 10:12–13, will remain there "waiting till His enemies are made His footstool." The Holy Spirit, however, is active and present and commissioned to interact with us on the earth today. As we've just seen, Jesus went away so the Spirit could come to us and live *in* us. He leads us into all truth, shows us things to come, reveals heavenly mysteries, and imparts vital direction.

The main reason many people aren't sure if they can really hear the voice of God is because they have refused to engage and embrace the member of the Trinity whose job it is to speak to them.

## OTHER WAYS THE SPIRIT HELPS

Let's look at John 16:8–11. In these four verses Jesus gives additional detail about how the Holy Spirit helps us. In fact, He mentions three more key aspects to the Helper's ministry. Let's look at the whole passage and then analyze it one piece at a time:

> And when He has come, He will convict the world of sin, and of
> righteousness, and of judgment: of sin, because they do not believe

in Me; of righteousness, because I go to My Father and you see Me
no more; of judgment, because the ruler of this world is judged.

### Conviction

Jesus names three areas in which the Holy Spirit will "convict" the world:
sin, righteousness, and judgment. What does Jesus mean by the word *convict*? To our modern ears this word conjures up thoughts of a criminal
prosecution. However, Jesus is talking about conviction in the sense of
"belief" or "persuasion." Simply put, to convict means to convince. And in
this role of helping, the Holy Spirit will convince the world of God's truths
concerning sin, righteousness, and judgment. He will persuade people that
certain things are true.

In verse 9, Jesus says the Holy Spirit will convict the world "of sin,
because they do not believe in Me." We need to understand that when the
Holy Spirit convicts lost people of sin—in other words, *convinces* them
that sin is ruling their lives—that's a good thing! This conviction is the
only way people become aware that
they need the Savior. The truth is that
no one ever comes to believe in Jesus
as Savior without first coming to the
conviction that he or she needs the
Savior. That's the Holy Spirit's job.

> We **NEED** to understand that **WHEN** the Holy Spirit **CONVICTS** lost people of sin, that's a **GOOD** thing!

I was saved in a shabby little
motel room. Of course, you don't
have to be in church to be saved. After
all, you're probably not going to die in a funeral home. It's convenient if you
do, but it probably won't happen. More than anything else, during that life-changing moment in a run-down motel, I remember the conviction of the
Holy Spirit. I'd been in church my whole life, but in that encounter I was
completely and thoroughly convinced—to the very core of my being—
that I was a sinner and needed Jesus. That conviction was the ministry of
the Holy Spirit, and I am more grateful than words can express that He
brought it to my life.

Think about the hour you were saved. Do you remember the conviction, your overwhelming sense of need? That was the Holy Spirit leading you to Jesus! In fact, 1 Corinthians 12:3 says that "no one can declare that Jesus is Lord except by the Holy Spirit."

### Righteousness

The Holy Spirit also convicts us of righteousness. Before we explore this particular ministry of the Holy Spirit, we need to have a clear understanding of what the word *righteousness* means. Contrary to common belief, righteousness doesn't mean "right behavior." Perhaps you've even heard someone with high moral standards referred to as "a righteous person." Of course, it's good to have high moral standards, but that's not righteousness. Instead, righteousness means having a "right standing" with God.

Please note that this verse doesn't say the Holy Spirit will convict us of the need for righteous living. While a right standing with God will indeed lead to righteous living, that's not the message in John 16:8–11. Rather, Jesus says the Holy Spirit will convict the world of righteousness because, "I go to My Father." The reason we can have a "right standing" before God is because Jesus ascended to the Father and sits at His right hand as an eternal reminder that our sins have been paid for (see Hebrews 10:8–14).

> Understanding that **YOU** have been made **RIGHTEOUS** is a wonderful **GIFT**.

When Jesus says the Holy Spirit will convict us of righteousness, He is referring to the fact that we all need to be convinced that righteousness exists —that it's even possible to have a right standing with God. In addition, once we're born again, the Holy Spirit's role is to convince us that we have been made righteous through the blood of Jesus Christ. He helps by providing an inner confidence of the wonderful reality of 2 Corinthians 5:21: "For [God] made Him who knew no sin to be sin for us, that we might become the righteousness of God in Him."

Understanding that you have been made righteous is a wonderful gift. The Holy Spirit helps you become fully convinced that you have a right standing with God, and you can come to His throne with confidence and the full assurance that you are received, welcomed, and embraced by Him.

## Judgment

Finally, the Holy Spirit was sent to convince the world of "judgment, because the ruler of this world is judged" (John 16:11).

To understand this aspect of the Holy Spirit's activity, we need to know who Jesus refers to as the "ruler of this world." A number of Bible passages establish that He is talking about Satan. For example, in John 12:31, Jesus says, "Now is the judgment of this world; now the ruler of this world will be cast out." In John 14:30, Jesus says, "I will no longer talk much with you, for the ruler of this world is coming, and he has nothing in Me."

This is clearly the enemy Jesus is talking about. Satan was the ruler of the world, but he was judged two thousand years ago through Jesus's sacrifice and subsequent victory over death, hell, and the grave. The Holy Spirit convicts us of this truth by convincing us that the former ruler of this world, Satan, has been judged and kicked out. He no longer has any authority in our lives. He's an outlaw.

## A PROPER UNDERSTANDING

It can be easy to misread and misunderstand the Holy Spirit's role. We've just looked at how the Holy Spirit comes to *convince* us of sin, righteousness, and judgment. But many people interpret these verses to mean the Holy Spirit's basic message is, "You're a horrible person. God is mad at you. And He's going to get you."

That's not the Holy Spirit's ministry at all! In fact, that is Satan's role. The Bible calls him "the accuser of our brethren" (Revelation 12:10). If you allow him, Satan will keep you feeling unworthy of God's acceptance and unwelcome in His presence by reminding you of every time you've blown it.

The Holy Spirit was sent to make us aware that we're lost and in need of Jesus; to lead us to Him; then to persuade us that we are in right standing with God through Him; and, finally, to fill us with the conviction that Satan is a defeated enemy who no longer has any authority over us.

When you open yourself to this ministry of the Holy Spirit, you'll find that He helps you in every area of your Christian life. That makes sense, because the Holy Spirit is our helper. But that's not all He is. He is also our friend, which we will explore next.

3

# Friend

I grew up in a small Texas town. As a typical small community in America, my hometown had a variety of churches. We also had Christian television. As a kid, these two things gave me a good exposure to different streams of Christianity.

My admittedly shallow, somewhat skeptical observations led me to conclude pretty early in life that Christians who talked a lot about the Holy Spirit generally fell into one of two groups: one in which the women didn't seem to wear any makeup at all, and the other in which they invariably wore way too much makeup. For a long time I figured that any woman who decided she wanted a deeper experience of the Holy Spirit faced a tough dilemma and had to ask herself, *Am I going to stop wearing makeup, or am I going to start wearing more?*

## THE LIES OF THE ENEMY

I am joking, of course. But these stereotypes are indeed alive and thriving today among huge numbers of Jesus-loving people. Many are sincerely reluctant to embrace the opportunity of a life-transforming relationship with the Holy Spirit because of such stereotypes.

Who do you think is the author of these misconceptions? It is Satan—the one who wants you to think that inviting the Holy Spirit into your life has little to do with friendship. He is the enemy who would convince you that giving the Spirit a larger role in your life will turn you into a weirdo.

Think about it. If the coming of the Helper, the Holy Spirit, is indeed a wonderful thing for believers, doesn't it make sense that the Enemy would want to keep us from experiencing that help? After all, one aspect of the Holy Spirit's work is to convince us that Satan has been judged and stripped of his authority. So is it really a stretch to think that Satan wants to keep us from receiving that conviction and acting on it?

I am convinced that one of Satan's primary strategies for keeping people from experiencing all the amazing help and benefits that come from a relationship with the Holy Spirit is to convince us that doing so will make us weird—*really weird*!

Of course, Satan has a lot of help in reinforcing that lie. The world has its share of truly eccentric people, and some of them are "Spirit-filled" Christians. But here's a news flash: they were weird before they were filled with the Spirit! That's just who they are. They'd be weird if they had never been saved and had pursued coin collecting instead. They would just be wacky coin collectors.

People sometimes do bizarre things and then claim that the Holy Spirit made them do it. He didn't. The Holy Spirit isn't weird. I know this is true because I know Him well. He's a good friend of mine.

This particular lie of the Enemy harms us more than we realize. On one hand we see all the biblical evidence that the Holy Spirit is a blessing and a helper. On the other hand the Enemy shows us goofy people doing goofy things in the name of the Spirit. As a result, we think, *This Holy Spirit stuff is probably good, but only in small doses. You just don't want to get too carried away with it.*

> The Holy Spirit
> **ISN'T WEIRD.**

In essence we tell the Holy Spirit, "Okay, I'll open the door of my life a few inches so You can stick Your foot in. But I'm not letting You come all the way in, because there's no telling what You'll do. I don't trust You to behave Yourself."

How insulting is that?

No! The Holy Spirit isn't strange. He is a wonderful, kind, and sensitive person. And a real friendship with Him can change your life.

## AMAZING BENEFITS

When the Holy Spirit becomes your friend, He brings four amazing benefits into your life. Let's look at these briefly.

### Power

Acts 1:8 says, "You shall receive power when the Holy Spirit has come upon you." Sadly, many Christians struggle all their days to live the Christian life, and they experience all kinds of failure, precisely because they try to live it in their own strength. They are saved, yet live lives of defeat and ineffectiveness, die, and go to heaven. But they spend their entire lives without ever using the only power that makes victorious living possible.

### Love

The Bible's famous "love chapter," 1 Corinthians 13, is sandwiched between two chapters that deal with the gifts of the Spirit. According to Romans 5:5, the Holy Spirit makes it possible for us to walk in the love of God toward others: "Now hope does not disappoint, because the love of God has been poured out in our hearts by the Holy Spirit who was given to us."

Perhaps the reason many Christians struggle and fail to walk in love is that they never open their hearts to the Holy Spirit, who holds the role of pouring out God's love within them. The great nineteenth-century evangelist Charles Finney described his life-changing encounter with the Holy Spirit this way:

> The Holy Spirit…seemed to go through me, body and soul…
> I could feel the impression, like a wave of electricity, going through
> and through me. Indeed it seemed to come in waves of liquid love,
> for I could not express it in any other way.*

---

* ChristianHistory.net, "Charles Finney: Father of American Revivalism," www.christianity today.com/ch/131christians/evangelistsandapologists/finney.html.

For Finney, this experience of God's love through the Holy Spirit was so transformative that the next day he quit his lucrative career as an attorney and started preaching full time. He went on to become one of the most influential revivalists in our nation's history.

### Fruit

According to Galatians 5:22, when we allow the Holy Spirit to fully dwell in our lives, He produces love, joy, peace, patience, kindness, gentleness, and a whole host of other good things. In fact, Paul opens this particular discussion about the Holy Spirit with the words, "I say then: Walk in the Spirit" (verse 16). And he closes it the same way with the words, "If we live in the Spirit, let us also walk in the Spirit" (verse 25).

As a pastor, I frequently encounter people who ask me the secret to being a person of greater peace or patience or gentleness or kindness. I tell them it's no secret. All those qualities and more are the natural by-products of enjoying the Holy Spirit's presence and fellowship. This is what Paul means by walking "in the Spirit."

### Gifts

The fruit of the Spirit is a gift. The qualities He produces in our lives are like packages from heaven itself, filled with blessings, miracles, and power.

> Is it any **WONDER** Satan is **TERRIFIED** by the thought of God's people **BECOMING** fully **OPEN** to the help of the Holy Spirit?

The earliest New Testament believers (see Acts 2) who threw the door open to the Holy Spirit turned the world upside down! Thousands came into the kingdom, miracles happened, and lives were transformed everywhere they went. Is it any wonder Satan is terrified by the thought of God's people becoming fully open to the help of the Holy Spirit? We shouldn't be surprised that the devil has done his best to make all this controversial.

However, abuse or misuse of any of the Spirit's gifts should never cause you to shy away from a full experience and a daily walk with the Holy Spirit, because you can't live a fully productive Christian life without Him.

I remember a story that comedian Bill Cosby told about his mother. She'd grown up amid great poverty, and when Bill and his three brothers were young, she scraped by on a meager housekeeper's salary while her husband was away in the navy. In later years Bill obviously became quite successful as an entertainer and could afford to buy his mother many nice things, which he did. But she wouldn't use them.

For example, Bill's mom had toast with breakfast every morning, but she would make it in her gas oven under the broiler. This was time consuming, inefficient, and even dangerous. Bill bought her a very nice toaster, which she left in the box and stuck on top of her refrigerator. He assumed she didn't like that brand of toaster, so he got her a different one. It also remained in the box and sat on the refrigerator. Soon she had three or four new, unused toasters sitting up there.

An exasperated Bill finally asked his mother why she refused to use the gifts he gave her. Her response was, "Leave them on the refrigerator. I'm used to doing it the old way."

That's exactly how many Christians respond to the gifts of the Spirit. They're comfortable doing it the old way. As a result, their lives are much more difficult and much less effective for the kingdom of God than they otherwise could be.

## THE FRIENDSHIP OF THE SPIRIT

Missing out on the gifts the Spirit brings is unfortunate. However, missing out on His friendship is tragic. I discovered this truth in an unusual way early in my Christian life.

I wasn't born again when Debbie and I first got married. Nine months after I made Debbie my wife, I made Jesus my Lord and experienced Him as Savior. While this was a powerful and transforming event, I still had a lot of emotional issues for which I needed healing and restoration. For one, I was insecure and even afraid of other people. I usually put on an outer show of confidence, but it was always a thin facade of cockiness covering a large amount of low self-esteem.

When we were first married, I used to dread Debbie's dragging me to Christmas parties. She naturally has a happy and outgoing personality, and she would invariably run off to chat with a friend while I was left to fend for myself.

> Something **REMARKABLE** happened when I entered into a real, **PERSONAL**, and dynamic relationship with the **HOLY SPIRIT**.

At the end of the night, when we got in the car to go home, I'd be upset with her. She couldn't understand why. She didn't know she had done anything wrong because, of course, she hadn't.

But I would get a pathetic tone in my voice and say, "You left me!"

"What do you mean, Robert? I was there all night!"

"You left me. And I was all alone. And...and people came up to me... and talked to me. It was horrible."

We're talking about a grown man here!

However, something remarkable happened when I entered into a real, personal, and dynamic relationship with the Holy Spirit.

I remember the first time we went to one of those dreaded social gatherings after my friendship with the Holy Spirit began. There I was, standing alone with a glass of punch in my hand and thinking, *She did it to me again. She's off chatting away, and here I am—alone and defenseless.* Then I heard the voice of the Holy Spirit clearly inside of me, saying, *I'm here, Robert, and you're not alone!*

The Holy Spirit and I started a conversation, one of the first of more than I can count. On this night, when the Spirit spoke, my eyes noticed a man across the room. The Holy Spirit said, *Do you see that man? He got a very bad report from his doctor the other day. He's afraid he's going to die and leave his young family destitute. You could pray for him.* So I did.

Next I noticed a silver-haired woman, and the Holy Spirit commented, *She lost her husband a few months ago. She's battling loneliness and crushing grief. Let's pray for her.*

At one point a man walked up and started a conversation. Instead of looking for a window to climb out of, I asked the Holy Spirit to use me to bless or help this person. The Holy Spirit prompted me to ask him about an area of his life that seemed quite personal. Still, I obeyed His prompting and said, "Are you doing okay with…?" and then mentioned what the Holy Spirit had revealed to me. The man looked at me in shock for a few seconds and then began to cry. I had the humble privilege of praying for him and giving him some desperately needed encouragement.

What's more, I didn't interact with this gentleman in a way that made me seem weird or made him feel humiliated. That's not the way of the Holy Spirit! I can say this from my experience with Him: He is gentle and kind. Wherever He is allowed to work, encouragement, light, life, and healing come.

## How the Spirit Speaks

One Sunday I had just concluded my message and invited those who wanted to receive Christ or needed prayer to come forward to the altar. A number of people were responding to that call, but my eyes fell upon one gentleman in particular. To my knowledge, I had never seen him before, and there was nothing about his facial expression or manner that would indicate why he was coming forward.

Nevertheless, as I looked at him, I heard the familiar voice of the Holy Spirit telling me something. I knew from experience that the Spirit reveals such things only because He wants to heal, restore, encourage, and bless. So I stepped toward the man and said, "Sir, as you were coming forward, the Lord told me something He wants you to know. He told me that you feel like the prodigal son, because you have been away from Him for a very long time. He just wanted me to give you a message from Him—'Welcome home, son.'"

Instantly the man's eyes filled with tears, and he fell into my arms. On behalf of the father who ran out to meet the returning prodigal of Jesus's parable, I put him in a bear hug that depicted in tangible terms the loving, forgiving embrace that awaits every person who turns to God.

What I did not know was that this was the man's first time inside the walls of a church in nearly twenty years. As he told me later, he had been raised in a Christian home and had given his life to Jesus as a boy. His Christian wife had been praying for him. But he had strayed and been running from God for a long, long time. True to form, the Enemy had been lying to him and telling him God would not receive him if he returned: *You've done too much. You've been too sinful. God has given up on you.*

> And because the **HOLY SPIRIT** still **SPEAKS**, it was my **PRIVILEGE** to bring him a very specific, amazingly **REDEMPTIVE** word from a **LOVING** heavenly Father.

So nervous was he about his return to church that while driving there he pulled over into an empty parking lot. When his wife asked him what was wrong, he turned to her and said, "I'm like the prodigal son. But I just don't know if God will really have me back. I'm afraid." With some encouragement from her, he continued on to the service. And because the Holy Spirit still speaks, it was my privilege to bring him a very specific, amazingly redemptive word from a loving heavenly Father.

When I mention without hesitation that the Holy Spirit speaks to me, I know some people probably find that weird as well. At the very least, people wonder, *Does the Holy Spirit really speak so clearly and directly?*

When we briefly explored this question earlier, I pointed out that the simple answer is yes: the Holy Spirit wants to speak clearly to us just as much as we want to hear clearly from Him. With that said, however, I want to give you some keys to hearing the voice of the Spirit. If you know how He talks, then you can know how to listen.

### The Holy Spirit Speaks Through His Word

First, the Holy Spirit is a person. We shouldn't think of our relationship with Him as anything more complicated than a relationship with any other person. When you meet new people and want to build relationships with them, you have to get to know them. You gradually learn about their backgrounds, their likes and dislikes, their habits and passions. The more you learn about them, the better you know them. The same is true with the Holy Spirit.

What if the person you just met had written a book about his life? If you wanted to know what he was all about, wouldn't it make sense to read what he'd written? The Holy Spirit was the inspiration behind every word of the Bible. So the starting point for a relationship with Him is the Word. In its pages we learn how God walks, talks, thinks, and acts. As we read and study Scripture, we discover His personality and character. If you want to get to know God, you have to read His Word.

> The Holy Spirit was
> the **INSPIRATION**
> behind every **WORD**
> of the **BIBLE**.

Pouring out your heart to God in prayer is the way you can talk to God. But renewing your mind by reading His Word is the most basic way you can allow God to talk to you.

### The Holy Spirit Speaks Through His Voice

In addition to speaking through His Word, God also speaks to individuals. He hasn't been giving His people the silent treatment for the past two thousand years! Hebrews 13:8 tells us that God doesn't change; He "is the same yesterday, today, and forever." This being true, why is it so hard to accept that God is still talking to us today?

Jesus Himself talked about the voice of the Spirit:

Most assuredly, I say to you, he who does not enter the sheepfold by the door, but climbs up some other way, the same is a thief and a robber. But he who enters by the door is the shepherd of the sheep. To him the doorkeeper opens, and the sheep hear his voice; and he calls his own sheep by name and leads them out. And when he brings out his own sheep, he goes before them; and the sheep follow him, for they know his voice. Yet they will by no means follow a stranger, but will flee from him, for they do not know the voice of strangers....

My sheep hear My voice, and I know them, and they follow Me. (John 10:1–5, 27)

Five times in these verses, Jesus refers either to the shepherd talking or to the sheep hearing the shepherd's voice. The sheep don't just hear his word; they hear his *voice*. We are Jesus's sheep, and according to His Word, we can and should hear His voice—the voice of the Spirit. When we hear it, we should know it.

Debbie and I were married in 1980, but we've known each other since elementary school. Once in a while she'll call me from a phone number I don't recognize on caller ID. On those occasions, when I answer the call and cautiously say, "Hello?" I hear a voice on the other end say, "Hey!" .

> **WE** are Jesus's **SHEEP**, and according to His **WORD**, we can and should **HEAR** His **VOICE**.

That single word is all I need. My voice and inflection instantly change to one expressing affection and familiarity. Without hesitation I respond, "Hey, honey. How are you?" I know the voice of my sweet bride. I've been listening to it for more than thirty years. After all the time we've spent together, talking and just living, I know her voice better than anyone else's on earth.

We can know the voice of the Spirit that well too. We can instantly recognize His voice beyond any doubt when He calls our names and speaks direction or encouragement to us. And don't think that the Holy Spirit only speaks to "important" or superspiritual sheep in the Shepherd's flock. You can know God's voice and hear Him just as clearly as the most famous evangelist hears Him.

We can come boldly before the throne of God through the access purchased for us through the blood of Jesus. And we can come to know His voice of reply, because Jesus sent the Holy Spirit to speak on behalf of the Father and the Son. Anytime you meet someone who really knows the voice of God, you quickly realize that person has spent a lot of time with Him.

Getting in God's presence—dwelling there, living there, and listening there—is the way to practice hearing God's voice.

In the early phases of this learning process, many believers say that the voice of the Spirit sounds a lot like their own thoughts or their own self-talk. There's a reason for this. When the Holy Spirit wants to get a message to you, He must communicate to your born-again human spirit and from there to your mind. So you're not likely to hear an audible voice. Instead, it comes as a *thought*. So it's easy to question whether the message is your own thought or something the Spirit is telling you.

> Don't **THINK** that the Holy Spirit **ONLY** speaks to "important" or **SUPERSPIRITUAL SHEEP** in the Shepherd's **FLOCK**.

With time and familiarity, however, you can learn to clearly distinguish between thoughts that are your own and those that come from the Spirit. The Shepherd still speaks to His sheep, calling us by name. Keep spending time with Him so that the next time He whispers, *Hey,* in your ear, you won't have to look at the caller ID. You'll know right away that God is speaking to you. The more you hear, recognize, and acknowledge His voice, the easier it will become to hear Him every time He speaks.

What an amazing privilege to have the Holy Spirit with and in us. He can be a trusted friend who wants to make everything better. And as we're about to discover, the opportunity to have this member of the Trinity as an ever-present friend is a privilege beyond human comprehension.

# 4

# God

o you remember the story I told earlier about my pastor's final words of advice as I was leaving for Bible college? He told me, "Watch out for people who talk about the Holy Spirit."

I don't mean to pick on him—although I've now referred to his words twice. I do know he was a good man and he loved the Lord. And I have no doubt that if I had asked him if he believed that the Holy Spirit was a member of the Trinity and just as much "God" as the Father or the Son, he would have instantly answered, "Absolutely!"

Yet, his words of warning revealed something about his attitude. In a very real sense, it's as if he told me, "Watch out for people who talk about God." In fact, as I was growing up, our church tradition tended to skip over Bible verses that referred to the Holy Spirit and His gifts. And for some reason, we never got around to studying many chapters in the book of Acts. Perhaps your church was like this too.

If so, it's possible that you don't see the Holy Spirit fully as God. Without even knowing it, you've accepted a subtle and incorrect teaching that the Holy Spirit is some kind of second-class member of the Trinity.

In a way, none of this should surprise us because the Holy Spirit never talks about or brings attention to Himself. The Holy Spirit only wants to talk about Jesus and see the Son lifted up. When Jesus introduces the Holy Spirit to His disciples in John 16, He says, "He will glorify Me, for He will take of what is Mine and declare it to you" (verse 14). In other words, a major part of the Holy Spirit's mission is revealing heavenly things that glorify

Jesus. *Isn't He wonderful?* the Holy Spirit says. *His earthly life was so amazing; His sacrifice was so enormous; His victory was so overwhelming; Jesus is so worthy of glory and honor and power and dominion.*

However, even though the Holy Spirit doesn't toot His own horn, we shouldn't think that He isn't a full and equal member of the Godhead. He is the third person of the Trinity. The Holy Spirit is God.

·

## SCRIPTURE REVEALS THE TRINITY

Verses throughout the Bible point to the Trinity—showing the Father, Son, and Holy Spirit in the same verse. Let's explore a few of these.

Earlier we looked at John 14:16, where Jesus says, "And I will pray the Father, and He will give you another Helper, that He may abide with you forever." Here the *Son* asks the *Father* to give the *Holy Spirit.* Several verses later, we see a similar description: "But the Helper, the Holy Spirit, whom the Father will send in My name, He will teach you all things" (verse 26). The *Holy Spirit* will be sent by the *Father* in the name of the *Son.*

In John 15, Jesus says, "But when the Helper comes, whom I shall send to you from the Father, the Spirit of truth who proceeds from the Father, He will testify of Me" (verse 26). The *Helper (the Spirit)* will be sent from the *Father* to testify of *Jesus (the Son).*

I'm sure you can see the pattern here. The Father, Son, and Spirit—one, yet three—working together.

This pattern appears throughout Scripture. For example, in Luke 3 we read the account of Jesus's baptism: "And the Holy Spirit descended in bodily form like a dove upon Him, and a voice came from heaven which said, 'You are My beloved Son; in You I am well pleased'" (verse 22). In a single moment the *Spirit* comes down upon the *Son* while the *Father* delivers an audible message of endorsement and praise. Speaking of baptism, in Matthew 28:19 we find part of Jesus's final instructions to His disciples prior to His ascension: "Go therefore and make disciples of all the nations, baptizing them in the name of the Father and of the Son and of the Holy Spirit."

The witness of Scripture is that the Holy Spirit is a full and equal member of the Trinity. The Holy Spirit is not a force, a thing, or an it. The Holy

Spirit is God in one of His three persons. Treating Him as some sort of heavenly afterthought or a lower order of supernatural being we can choose to ignore is grievous. Take a sobering look at Acts 5, where we have the account of the apostle Peter exposing the deception of Ananias and Sapphira. In verse 3, Peter says, "Ananias, why has Satan filled your heart to lie to the Holy Spirit?" Now notice the words that come out of Peter's mouth in the next verse: "You have not lied to men but to God" (verse 4).

Yes, when you lie to the Holy Spirit, you lie to God.

## CONNECTING US TO THE FATHER AND SON

By now you're probably wondering why I am spending so much time making a case that the Holy Spirit is part of the Trinity. I'm dwelling on it because we can easily acknowledge in our minds that the Holy Spirit is God, yet display a very different belief in our actions and attitudes. The more we understand what a wonderful, helpful, and amazing person the Holy Spirit is, the more we realize that our incorrect attitudes about Him are a tragedy and an offense.

My experience of the Holy Spirit has consistently been one of a person who looks for ways to help the hurting and connect them with a Father who loves them and the Savior who died for them. Here's an example of what I'm talking about.

I recall a time when I was invited to be a guest minister at a church where I didn't really know anyone in the congregation. I was sitting on the platform, waiting to speak. As we were singing and worshiping, I looked out at the

> At that **INSTANT** I heard the **FAMILIAR** voice of the Holy Spirit **SPEAK** something **TO ME** about her.

people and my eyes fell upon a particular woman. At that instant I heard the familiar voice of the Holy Spirit speak something to me about her.

When it was time for me to preach, I walked to the pulpit and spoke directly to her. "Ma'am, would you stand up for a moment?" I said. "When we were worshiping, the Holy Spirit pointed you out to me. He said to me, 'Robert, do you know her past?'"

When I said that, the woman's countenance fell, and she began staring at the floor. But I wasn't finished. I said, "Yes, the Holy Spirit asked me if I knew your past, and I said, 'No, Lord, I don't.' And the Holy Spirit immediately said, 'Hmm...neither do I.'"

At that she lifted up her head and began to smile. "You know, ma'am," I said, "I know God knows everything. But He told me to tell you that He has chosen not to remember your past. He has forgotten it. And He says it's time for you to do the same."

She wept and laughed, as did many of her friends in the congregation.

I believe this story embodies what the Holy Spirit is all about. He values too highly the awesome sacrifice made by the Father and the Son to provide forgiveness of our sins to allow one of His children to live in unnecessary shame. The Holy Spirit is a kind, compassionate, wonderful, sensitive person.

And He is God.

## Summing Up

What is the Holy Spirit saying to you so far as we've explored who He is? What's the state of your relationship with Him? Let me challenge you to make an honest assessment of that in your heart. Have the courage to ask yourself some pointed questions.

Are you a little afraid of the Holy Spirit? Have you seen some bad examples—some misuses or abuses—that have caused you to keep your heart closed to the ministry of the Holy Spirit? Have they caused you to shrink back when you've sensed the presence or promptings of the Holy Spirit?

If so, I encourage you to realize three truths before we go further on this journey: (1) the Holy Spirit was sent to be your helper, (2) He wants to be your intimate friend, and (3) the truth that makes those two statements most amazing of all is *He is God.*

PART 2

# What Is This Person Like?

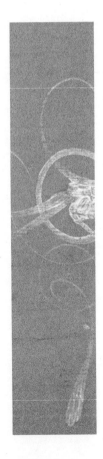

# 5

# His Personality

I have a favorite chair. I really love it. But it doesn't love me back. In fact, I can't have a relationship with it at all.

Notice that I called my chair an "it." Most of us learned in our earliest English classes that the pronoun *it* refers to something that isn't a person. Yet people frequently use this pronoun when speaking of the Holy Spirit. How many times have you heard someone say something along the lines of, "You know the Holy Spirit, *it's* like the wind," or, "We need more of *it* in our lives"?

This kind of language reveals a mind-set that the Holy Spirit isn't a person but rather some sort of impersonal force. This is a common view. In fact, whole theological systems have been built around the premise that the Holy Spirit doesn't have personhood. Even in the early centuries of the church, a heretical movement called Arianism denied the personhood of the Holy Spirit. In our day the Jehovah's Witnesses sect believes the same thing.

However, this view presents a big problem. If you don't see the Holy Spirit as a *person,* you'll never develop a *personal* relationship with Him. Why? Because you don't develop a personal relationship with a thing or an object. I've never thought about sharing my feelings with my favorite chair, and I've never struck up a conversation with a tree in my backyard.

We can only experience the amazing benefits and joys that come with a friendship with the Holy Spirit when we fully understand that He is a person.

## A Name or a Role?

I'm a deep thinker. Of course, *deep* is a relative term. Nevertheless, I've spent a lot of time pondering the question of why people have no trouble viewing the Father or Jesus as persons, yet consistently think of the Holy Spirit as a thing. As is often the result when I have deep thoughts, I have come up with some ideas for helping God improve His methods. It occurred to me that the reason some people don't think of the Holy Spirit as a person lies in His name, *the* Holy Spirit.

So, I told Him, "Lord, I was thinking it probably would have been better if the third member of the Trinity had been named something like Bill. If He had a regular name, we could say, 'I'm going to get Bill's advice on this matter,' rather than religiously pronouncing, 'I plan to seek the guidance of the Holy Spirit.'"

The more I thought about this, the more brilliant it seemed. If this plan were adopted, formal churches could call Him "William" and still feel proper. Churches a little more on the wild side could call Him "Billy." My idea would offer something for everyone, and it would end the tendency to view the Holy Spirit as a thing.

Of course, I'm just kidding. But at the root of my little joke is a serious truth: the names we use to refer to three members of the Trinity can add to the confusion about the Holy Spirit's personhood. However, the term *the Holy Spirit* isn't a name. It's a description of His role, just like *Father* and *Son* describe specific roles. These words describe the functions of the three members of the Trinity: "God, the Father," "God, the Son," and "God, the Holy Spirit." Some of the confusion comes because the terms *father* and *son* naturally cause us to think of persons, but the term *spirit* doesn't.

## What Is Personhood?

If we want to have a real friendship with the Holy Spirit, we must get rid of our confusion and start seeing God the Holy Spirit as a person.

How can we know for sure He is a person? Well, how do we know anyone is a person? What constitutes personhood? Some people might say, "A person has life." Well, a tree has life too. But the last time I checked, a tree isn't a person.

Let me offer a simple definition of personhood first and then follow it with a slightly more complex one.

Simply speaking, a *person* is a being with a *personality.* All persons exhibit the marks of a personality. If something doesn't have a personality, it's not a person as we understand the term.

Now let me present a more intricate answer. A person is a being with a soul.

Interestingly, the idea that God has a soul can seem a little strange. However, Scripture tells us that He does. In Matthew 12:18, God the Father speaks and says of Jesus, "Behold! My Servant whom I have chosen, My Beloved in whom *My soul* is well pleased!" That's pretty clear! We might not think about God the Father having a soul, but He does.

What about God the Son? Matthew 26:38 says this concerning Jesus: "Then He said to them, '*My soul* is exceedingly sorrowful.'" That's pretty clear as well. Why would Jesus say "My soul" if He doesn't have one?

We're two-for-two on souls in the Trinity. So what about the Holy Spirit? In Hebrews 10:38 the Spirit of grace declares, "Now the just shall live by faith; but if anyone draws back, *My soul* has no pleasure in him."

God the Father, God the Son, and God the Holy Spirit all have a soul, and all fit the definition of personhood. A person's soul is made up of three components: mind, will, and emotions. In other words, a person who has a soul has thoughts, makes choices, and has feelings. The capacity to do these three things indicates the presence of a soul. Let's apply this three-part test to God.

Think about the dozens of Scripture passages that refer to "the mind of God." Now think about the dozens and dozens of passages that refer to "the will of God." Finally, think about all the verses that mention God's feelings or emotions. Throughout the Bible, we see God experiencing joy, sadness, anger, and pleasure.

Clearly, God has a mind, a will, and emotions. This means He has a soul. And this is true for God the Father, God the Son, and God the Holy Spirit. (We'll discuss the Spirit's soul at length in the chapters that follow.)

> Clearly, **GOD** has a mind, a will, and **EMOTIONS**.

As Christians, we have Someone living within us who *is* God. He has the mind of God, He knows the will of God, and He knows God's feelings. He resides within us because He wants to help us think the way God thinks, desire what God desires, and feel what God feels. What a privilege!

## God's Attributes

As a person in the Trinity, the Holy Spirit possesses all the attributes that God has. When you begin to study the attributes of God, you find a deep and many-faceted subject. Understanding these attributes can help us see that the Holy Spirit is indeed a person, not a force or a thing. The list of God's attributes is long. But at the top of the list, you'll likely find three attributes that begin with the prefix *omni*. Let's look at these briefly.

### Omniscient

God is "all knowing." The theological term for this is *omniscience.* The term is a combination of two words: *omni,* which means "all," and *science,* which comes from a Latin word meaning "knowledge." Someone who is omniscient is all knowing—simply knowing everything there is to know. I once read a more complete definition that defined omniscience as "the attribute of God by which God perfectly and eternally knows all things which can be known, past, present, and future."*

Think about the wealth and breadth of God's knowledge. You might have a great set of encyclopedias at home, and the Internet gives us access to a mind-numbing amount of information. Yet these collections of information

---

* The Parent Company, "God Is Omniscient," www.parentcompany.com/awareness_of_god/aog12.htm.

have nothing on God. Psalm 147:4 declares that God not only knows how many stars there are, but He also has a name for each one. In Psalm 33:13 we learn that God has the capacity to see and know every person on the face of the earth, all at the same time. His knowledge of each of us is so intimate, He even knows the ever-changing number of hairs on our heads (see Matthew 10:30).

God also knows the innermost thoughts of our hearts and minds. No knowledge is hidden from Him. This is just as true for God the Holy Spirit as it is for God the Father.

### Omnipotent

God is also *omnipotent,* which means "all powerful." In Jeremiah 32, God asks Jeremiah, "Behold, I am the LORD, the God of all flesh. Is there anything too hard for Me?" (verse 27). Of course, God asked the prophet a rhetorical question. The correct answer is no. Nothing is too hard for God. The angel Gabriel affirms this truth personally when he speaks to the Virgin Mary and says, "Nothing is impossible for God!" (Luke 1:37, CEV).

God's omnipotence also means that no one can thwart His plans. Whatever He purposes to do, He does. What He wants done, gets done. That's why Job says, "I know that You can do everything, and that no purpose of Yours can be withheld from You" (Job 42:2). And the psalmist says, "Our God is in heaven; He does whatever He pleases" (Psalm 115:3).

> **NOTHING** is too **HARD** for God.

The apostle Paul speaks specifically of God the Holy Spirit when he says, "Now to Him who is able to do exceedingly abundantly above all that we ask or think, according to the power that works in us" (Ephesians 3:20). There are a number of important truths about God's power and sovereignty revealed in this verse:

(1) He is able to *do* or to work (*poiēsai*), for he is neither idle, nor inactive, nor dead. (2) He is able to do what *we ask,* for he hears and answers prayer. (3) He is able to do what we ask *or think,* for he reads

our thoughts, and sometimes we imagine things for which we dare not and therefore do not ask. (4) He able to do *all* that we ask or think, for he knows it all and can perform it all. (5) He is able to do *more...than* (*hyper,* "beyond") all that we ask or think, for his expectations are higher than ours. (6) He is able to do much more, or *more abundantly* (*perissōs*), than all that we ask or think, for he does not give his grace by calculated measure. (7) He is able to do very much more, *far more abundantly,* than all that we ask or think, for he is a God of super-abundance.*

Note that Paul says this ability and power "works in us." The source of that power is God the Holy Spirit. My best friend is omnipotent.

## Omnipresent

God is also *omnipresent,* which means He is simultaneously everywhere. I've always found it comforting to know that no matter where I go, the God who loves me is already present. No place in heaven or on earth is beyond the reach of His love and care. That's the truth the psalmist expresses so beautifully in Psalm 139:

> Where can I go from Your Spirit?
>> Or where can I flee from Your presence?
> If I ascend into heaven, You are there;
>> If I make my bed in hell, behold, You are there.
> If I take the wings of the morning,
>> And dwell in the uttermost parts of the sea,
> Even there Your hand shall lead me,
>> And Your right hand shall hold me. (verses 7–10)

In addition, God's omnipresence means that He transcends not only space but also time. God isn't just every*where* at once; He is every *when* at once as well. Because He stands outside of time, He not only sees your

---

* John R. W. Stott, *The Message of Ephesians (The Bible Speaks Today)* (Downer's Grove: InterVarsity, 1979), 139–40.

present moment and circumstances, He also sees your past and future. Of course, He graciously chooses to forget the sinful parts of our pasts that we confess and place under the blood of Jesus.

> **GOD** isn't just **EVERYWHERE** at once; He is every **WHEN** at once as well.

When you begin to cultivate a relationship with the Holy Spirit and learn to hear His voice, it's exciting to realize that He knows the future. The Holy Spirit knows when danger waits around the corner and will warn you if you'll listen. He also knows when great opportunities lie ahead and will help you be ready to seize them.

My friend Dr. Tony Evans has a great way of expressing how all these attributes work together. He says,

> There is nothing God does not know; that's His omniscience....
> There is no place where He does not exist; that's His omnipresence.
> But that's not all. There is nothing God cannot do; that's His omnipotence.*

All three members of the Godhead have all three of these attributes. The Son, now sitting at the Father's right hand, knows everything the Father knows. The same is true for the Holy Spirit.

The Holy Spirit is certainly not an "it"! He has personality and a soul, and is a person who can be your best friend. With that in mind, let's learn more about the qualities of His soul.

---

* Tony Evans, *Time to Get Serious* (Wheaton, IL: Crossway, 1995), 22.

# 6

# His Soul: Mind and Will

I once heard a man who ministered to college students say that the two most well-attended seminar topics at Christian conferences are "How to Know God's Will for Your Life" and "Sex and Dating." He joked that if he really wanted a large crowd for his seminars, he'd call them "How to Know God's Will Concerning Sex and Dating."

More than anything else, Christians struggle and long to know God's will for their lives. In fact, surveys reveal that the number one spiritual question believers ask is, "How can I know the will of God?"

The reason more Christians don't know the will of God is that they don't have a friendship with the Holy Spirit—the One inside them whose job it is to reveal all truth to them.

Let me repeat that.

You have Someone living in you who knows the will of God for your life. If you want to get to know the will of God, get to know the Holy Spirit. Your friendship with Him can truly change your life. As we've been exploring, a friendship with the Holy Spirit is possible because He is a person. Of course, He is God, but we've also seen that the respective members of the Trinity each have the attributes of a soul. Having a soul means possessing three things—a mind, a will, and emotions.

We can get our minds around this truth concerning God the Son. We know Jesus has a soul because we see His personality displayed throughout the Gospels. We see Him laugh, cry, become exasperated, show compassion, choose, teach, encourage, and love. At the heart of the miracle of the

Incarnation is the amazing reality that Jesus became one of us! As the apostle John writes, "The Word became flesh and dwelt among us" (John 1:14). Paul depicts Jesus as "taking the form of a bondservant, and coming in the likeness of men. And being found in appearance as a man, He humbled Himself and became obedient to the point of death, even the death of the cross" (Philippians 2:7–8).

While we can easily conclude that Jesus has a soul, few of us think about the Holy Spirit in these terms. Yet we need to understand that the Holy Spirit has a soul if we want to enjoy the blessings of friendship with Him. As we discussed earlier, no one tries to have a relationship with a thing—at least no rational person does.

With that in mind, let's dig a little deeper into Scripture that helps us see that the Spirit has a mind, a will, and emotions—the elements of His soul.

## The Mind of the Holy Spirit

Let's begin with the familiar words of Isaiah 55:

> "For My thoughts are not your thoughts,
>     Nor are your ways My ways," says the Lord.
> "For as the heavens are higher than the earth,
>     So are My ways higher than your ways,
>     And My thoughts than your thoughts." (verses 8–9)

God's own words here are pretty convincing. Why would He say, "My thoughts are not your thoughts" if He doesn't have thoughts? And how can He have thoughts if He doesn't have a mind? God indeed does have a mind, and He thinks about you and your situations. Wouldn't you like to know what His thoughts are?

We've already seen that one of the roles of the Holy Spirit is to "guide [us] into all truth" (John 16:13). It only makes sense that if the Holy Spirit will guide you into all truth, He must know all truth. Of course, because the Holy Spirit is God, He is omniscient. You'll remember that this attribute of

God means He is all knowing. The bottom line is that God the Holy Spirit possesses all knowledge.

Have you ever wondered about the intelligence quotient of God? Albert Einstein's IQ was measured at 209. That's pretty impressive. But what about God's IQ? Before you venture a guess, let me tell you that God doesn't have an IQ. Why? The term *quotient* implies both a calculation and a comparison. However, God's intelligence can't be calculated, and nothing exists to which it can be compared. It's immeasurable. When it comes to IQ, God has no *Q*. But He does have lots and lots of *I*.

> God's **INTELLIGENCE** can't be **CALCULATED**, and nothing exists to which it can be **COMPARED**.

When you start contemplating the wisdom and intelligence of God, you will have some pretty mind-blowing thoughts. For example, God is incapable of thinking of something He's never thought of before. If He could, He might learn something. But a God who knows everything has nothing to learn. Let me state it another way: Nothing has ever occurred to God. God has never slapped His forehead and said, "Do you know what I just thought of?" Never. He knows everything, all at once, all the time.

The amazing news is that you have the Holy Spirit living within you, and as God, He has that same level of wisdom and knowledge. The Holy Spirit knows everything about everything, and He has committed Himself to be your teacher. He promises to lead you into all truth. The One whose job description is "Helper" possesses all truth. He knows the answer to every problem you face. You have access to the mind of God, because the Holy Spirit has a mind.

In Romans 8, Paul says one of the Holy Spirit's roles is to intercede for us and help us when we don't know what or how to pray:

> Now He who searches the hearts *knows what the mind of the Spirit is,* because He makes intercession for the saints according to the will of God. (verse 27)

Both God the Father and God the Holy Spirit have a mind, and the Holy Spirit is able to intercede for us in accordance with the will of God.

## THE WILL OF THE HOLY SPIRIT

Let's look next at the second key element of the Holy Spirit's soul: He also has a will. Scripture provides abundant evidence for this truth. For example, in Acts 16 we find Paul traveling with Silas and Timothy. Paul plans to head into Asia Minor (modern-day Turkey) to preach the gospel. What could be wrong with taking the logical next step to tell lost people about Jesus? The plan faces just one problem. The Holy Spirit says, "Don't!"

> Now when they had gone through Phrygia and the region of Galatia, they were forbidden by the Holy Spirit to preach the word in Asia. (Acts 16:6)

This word translated "forbidden" in our English New Testaments is a Greek word that means "to exert one's will." In this instance the Holy Spirit simply exerts His will—which He can do because He has a will to exert.

As the One who knows all truth, who knows things to come, and who knows the mind of God the Father, the Holy Spirit knew that it would be outside of God's master plan for the spread of the gospel if Paul and his companions headed that direction. A time to evangelize that part of the world would come, but this wasn't it. How did Paul and Silas learn God's will about where to go? They recognized and heeded the voice of the Holy Spirit.

The Holy Spirit has a will, and that will is in perfect alignment with the will of the Father. Consider these additional insights about discovering the will of God.

### God's General Will

God's will consists of two realms. One is His general will for your life. The Bible is your infallible guide to God's general will. If you need to know about morality or behavioral boundaries, the Bible provides clear direction. You don't have to wonder whether or not it is God's will for you to not steal, to be faithful to your spouse, or to honor your parents. Scripture clearly states God's will in these areas. We call this His general will because these boundaries are true and apply to every person.

If you're married, God's general will helps you know how to treat your spouse. But His general will won't reveal whom you should marry in the first place. That question involves God's specific will for you. You won't find a Bible verse that says, "Behold, John Smith, thou shalt woo and wed Jane Doe of Upper Sandusky, Ohio. And ye shall make her thy bride, yea, a wedded wife thou shalt make of her."

> If you **NEED** to know about **MORALITY** or behavioral **BOUNDARIES**, the Bible provides **CLEAR** direction.

## God's Specific Will

So how can we know the specific will of God? Please get this powerful and important truth: we come to know the general will of God by His *Word,* while we come to know the specific will of God by His *voice.* Remember what Jesus told us about the Helper He would send:

> I still have many things to say to you, but you cannot bear them now. However, when He, the Spirit of truth, has come, He will guide you into all truth; for He will not speak on His own authority, but whatever He hears He will speak; and He will tell you things to come. (John 16:12–13)

The Holy Spirit speaks. He can speak to you. He *wants* to speak to you. I don't think we appreciate what an incredible privilege this is.

Before the Holy Spirit came two thousand years ago, entire generations of people existed where usually just one person per generation heard from God and could speak for God. Just one person! Read the Old Testament and you'll see that in their generations men like Samson, Samuel, Elijah, Elisha, Habakkuk, Nahum, Hosea, Joel, and Amos heard from God, but almost no one else did.

Even the kings of Judah depended on one or a small handful of prophets to find out what God wanted them to do. If you were a lowly citizen with no prophet of God nearby, you were on your own. In addition, during one four-hundred-year stretch between the Old and New Testaments, God spoke to no one.

> The **COMING** of the Holy Spirit **MARKS** a sharp **LINE** on the time line of **HISTORY**.

When the Holy Spirit arrived two thousand years ago, it was a game-changing event for humanity. As with Jesus's death and resurrection, the coming of the Holy Spirit marks a sharp line on the time line of history. Nothing has been the same since. Note what Peter stands up and says about the Spirit's arrival on the Day of Pentecost:

> But this is what was spoken by the prophet Joel:
> "And it shall come to pass in the last days, says God,
> That I will pour out of My Spirit on all flesh;
> Your sons and your daughters shall prophesy,
> Your young men shall see visions,
> Your old men shall dream dreams." (Acts 2:16–17)

The prophet Joel had predicted this history-changing event six hundred years earlier. Joel said that the Spirit of God Himself would be poured into human flesh, and young and old, male and female would be able to have visions and dreams from God in the way only a handful of Old Testament prophets had in the past. And now Peter is declaring the glorious arrival of the day when people can hear God for themselves. Why? Because the Holy Spirit had come.

Isn't that wonderful news? You can have a personal relationship with God through the person of the Holy Spirit! No intermediaries or go-betweens or hard-to-find prophets. You can't have a personal relationship with God through your pastor, your spouse, or any other person. You must have your own personal relationship with God through the Holy Spirit.

Imagine if someone came up to you and said, "Excuse me. I know you don't know me very well, but would you ask my wife where she wants to go on vacation this year?"

What would you say? Your response would likely be, "Um, no. She's *your* wife. *You* ask her where she wants to go on vacation."

What if the question was more personal: "Pardon me, stranger, would you please ask my wife how many children she wants us to have?" Of course, you'd probably answer even more emphatically, "No, that's something you should ask her yourself!"

I know these seem like ridiculous illustrations. Yet, because I'm a pastor, people approach me all the time hoping I will ask God about His will for their lives. My answer is always pretty much the same. I say, "No. He's your heavenly Father too. *You* ask Him!"

> You **MUST** have your **OWN** personal **RELATIONSHIP** with God through the **HOLY SPIRIT**.

Of course, I certainly believe in seeking wise counsel when making a decision. But that's not the same as expecting someone else to hear God's voice on your behalf because you can't or won't.

Remember, others can hear God *with* you but not *for* you. The Father and the Son sent the Holy Spirit so you can have a *personal* relationship with God.

I remember a time when a man approached me after a church service. He said, "Can you get a word from God for me?"

I looked at him in a startled sort of way for a moment and said, "Well, okay, if God tells me something concerning you, I'll pass it along. But I don't think that will happen."

The next day I was spending quiet time with the Lord, and I remembered the man and his request. I didn't want to ignore an opportunity if God wanted to minister to the man, so I offhandedly asked, "Lord, do You have something You want me to tell him?" Instantly, I heard the familiar voice of the Lord respond and say, *Yes. Tell him I want to talk to him personally. Tell him to be in My office first thing tomorrow morning!*

I can personally testify that individuals can hear the voice of the Holy Spirit—clearly, powerfully, and consistently. I've been living my life that way for years now.

He speaks to me about decisions and helps me choose more wisely than I ever could on my own. After all, He knows the future. Sometimes a path that seems prudent and safe on the surface can result in disaster. I can't tell you how many times I've been faced with a choice, yet when I submitted the situation to the Holy Spirit for guidance, He has directed me to take a less-likely path. His guidance has never failed to work out to my benefit.

> Remember, **OTHERS** can **HEAR** God *with* you but not *for* **YOU**.

The Spirit speaks to me about my family, helping me be the best husband and father possible.

He gently corrects me when I'm out of line and often makes me look much smarter and wiser than I am. He exposes the schemes and strategies of the Enemy—who would like nothing better than to destroy me—allowing me to thwart them before they can do damage.

The Holy Spirit speaks to me about people who cross my path each day. He gives me extraordinary opportunities to bless, encourage, and present Jesus to others. Some of the most rewarding and memorable moments of my life in ministry have occurred when the Holy Spirit gives me a special word to deliver to a stranger. When that happens, tears and healing and restoration and deliverance follow. I've been humbled yet privileged to be a part of these encounters with the grace and compassion of God.

God wants to speak to you personally too. He wants you to know His will and His wonderful fellowship. The way to know the will of God is to know God! The Holy Spirit has a mind and a will, and you can know His thoughts and His will—*if* you know Him.

# His Soul: Emotions

C an you and I make the Holy Spirit joyful or sad? We certainly can, and in a few pages I will tell of a time I distinctly disappointed my friend the Holy Spirit, then—after my repentance and God's forgiveness— saw the joy in our relationship wonderfully restored. But before I tell that story, I first want to describe the emotional makeup of the Holy Spirit.

Like any other person with a soul, the Holy Spirit also has emotions. Look at the list of "the fruit of the Spirit." These attributes arise in anyone who allows the Holy Spirit to express Himself in his or her life.

> The fruit of the Spirit is love, joy, peace, longsuffering, kindness,
> goodness, faithfulness, gentleness, self-control. (Galatians 5:22–23)

A tree can't love. It might be alive, but it will never experience joy. Only a person can experience peace. The same goes for kindness, goodness, faithfulness, gentleness, and self-control. These are characteristics of a person.

In the same way, only a person can feel the opposite of joy—grief. In Ephesians 4:30 we read this warning: "And do not grieve the Holy Spirit of God, by whom you were sealed for the day of redemption."

When you have an intimate friend, it's natural to want to know what makes him or her sad.

That's certainly the case with my wife, Debbie. Because she is also one of my best friends in the world, I've learned through the years what upsets her or causes her pain. Then I'm careful to avoid doing those things. Why?

Because I'm afraid of her? No, because I love her, and I treasure our relationship.

Some Christians are surprised to learn they can upset the Holy Spirit and cause Him grief or pain. Some of this surprise occurs because they don't view Him as a person who possesses a mind, a will, and emotions. However, once you start to value the relationship you have with Him, you'll care whether or not your actions bring Him pain. You naturally become interested in knowing what upsets your dear friend. You care because you love Him, and you hate the thought of creating distance between the two of you.

> Some Christians are **SURPRISED** to learn they can **UPSET** the Holy Spirit and **CAUSE** Him **GRIEF** or pain.

So just what is *grief*? Simply put, grief is sadness you feel at the loss of intimacy with someone. We traditionally associate grief with the death of someone we love, because death creates a break in intimacy with the person who dies. But our hurtful thoughts and actions can also cause a temporary loss of intimacy. So we must ask ourselves a key question: what grieves the Holy Spirit? We find some of the answer in the verses immediately around Ephesians 4:30. Let's look at the whole passage in context:

> Therefore, putting away lying, "Let each one of you speak truth with his neighbor," for we are members of one another. "Be angry, and do not sin": do not let the sun go down on your wrath, nor give place to the devil. Let him who stole steal no longer, but rather let him labor, working with his hands what is good, that he may have something to give him who has need. Let no corrupt word proceed out of your mouth, but what is good for necessary edification, that it may impart grace to the hearers. And do not grieve the Holy Spirit of God, by whom you were sealed for the day of redemption. Let all bitterness, wrath, anger, clamor, and evil speaking be put away from you, with all malice. And be kind to one another, tenderhearted, forgiving one another, even as God in Christ forgave you. (verses 25–32)

Notice some of the specific behaviors that cause the Spirit to grieve: lying, sin, stealing, neglecting to give to others. In fact, a pattern emerges in these verses. All these behaviors relate to how we treat others, particularly our brothers and sisters in Christ. For example, we are to put away lying because "we are members of one another." Because the Holy Spirit lives in every believer, mistreating any one of them involves mistreating the Holy Spirit in them. That's why verses 31–32 say, "Let all bitterness, wrath, anger, clamor, and evil speaking be put away from you, with all malice. And be kind to one another, tenderhearted, forgiving one another, even as God in Christ forgave you." In other words, stop mistreating one another. It grieves the Holy Spirit.

Sin doesn't grieve the Holy Spirit because He's a prude and doesn't want you to have fun. Sin grieves the Holy Spirit because sin hurts people and the Holy Spirit loves people. Further, when a believer walks in rebellion and willful sin, the Holy Spirit experiences grief because the rebellion creates a sudden loss of intimacy with a person He loves—even though that intimacy will eventually be restored.

As a believer, you don't lose your salvation when you sin, because your salvation is based on grace through faith. However, when you're in willful rebellion, you do interrupt your intimacy with the Holy Spirit—and that loss of connection with someone He loves produces grief in Him.

## BITTERNESS AND INIQUITY

In addition to the behaviors listed in Ephesians 4, I believe the Holy Spirit finds two things particularly grievous. We find those illustrated in Acts 8.

### Bitterness

In this passage, Peter and John travel to Samaria to minister to a group of believers who have been saved through the preaching of the evangelist Philip. When they arrive, they discover that these new believers haven't yet received any teaching about the Holy Spirit and know nothing about receiving His ministry in their lives.

John and Peter pray for these new believers to receive the Holy Spirit. When they do, a lot of miraculous things start to happen. When a famous local magician named Simon—who had been saved and baptized in this Samaritan revival—sees all the miracles taking place, he offers to buy this "power" from Peter:

> When Simon saw that through the laying on of the apostles' hands the Holy Spirit was given, he offered them money, saying, "Give me this power also, that anyone on whom I lay hands may receive the Holy Spirit." (Acts 8:18–19)

Of course, Peter is deeply offended at the thought that the power of God could be purchased. Peter says to him,

> Your money perish with you, because you thought that the gift of God could be purchased with money! You have neither part nor portion in this matter, for your heart is not right in the sight of God. Repent therefore of this your wickedness, and pray God if perhaps the thought of your heart may be forgiven you. For I see that you are poisoned by bitterness and bound by iniquity. (verses 20–23)

Notice that Simon's first mistake came when he relegated the *person* of the Holy Spirit to a *power* that he could buy like a commodity. He viewed the Holy Spirit as a *force* he could buy rather than a *person* he could know.

> Everything that **GRIEVES** the Holy Spirit involves **HOW** we **TREAT** one another.

Peter rebukes Simon sternly and ends his statement with a remarkable observation: "For I see that you are poisoned by bitterness and bound by iniquity."

As we've seen, everything that grieves the Holy Spirit involves how we treat one another. But we need to add an important truth to that understanding: if you have bitterness in any area of your life, you have poison in your system. Bitterness poisons you emotionally, spiritually, mentally, and physically.

For his entire life Simon had been the big man of supernatural power in that area. He was the wonder worker whose magic prompted "oohs" and "aahs." Of course, the source of his power as a sorcerer had been demonic rather than heavenly.

Simon watched the apostles turn the city upside down with miraculous signs and wonders. He lost all his former power when he was saved. Envy and jealousy ate at him until he finally tried to purchase the power of the Holy Spirit. Of course, the irony is that as a believer Simon already had the Spirit's power fully available to him! Jesus Himself had said that all the miraculous signs and wonders the disciples produced are really the normal fruit that follow people who believe in Him:

> And these signs will follow those who believe: In My name they will cast out demons; they will speak with new tongues; they will take up serpents; and if they drink anything deadly, it will by no means hurt them; they will lay hands on the sick, and they will recover. (Mark 16:17–18).

## Iniquity

In addition to bitterness Simon was also "bound by iniquity." We don't use the word *iniquity* in everyday conversation. This old-fashioned word refers to the bondage that habitual sin creates in your life. Sin is an event; iniquity is a lifestyle. Sin is an act; iniquity is a habit.

In Simon's case, his iniquity came from bondage to some type of immorality. This isn't surprising, because Simon had been yielding himself to demonic powers for most of his life. You don't play footsie with the devil for years without getting involved in some dark habits and practices.

We all carry baggage into our new lives in Christ, and Simon would have been no exception. You probably noticed that all your unclean habits didn't simply fall away the moment you asked Jesus into your life.

The Christian life is an upward journey. The moment we're born again, we are made *righteous*—put in right standing with God. But *sanctification*—becoming pure and more Christlike in our behavior—is a process. The Holy Spirit wants to be our partner and friend in that process. That's why we grieve the Spirit when we allow a stronghold of iniquity to remain once He has brought it to our attention. Of course, some iniquities are shallow and have a weak hold on us. However, others have roots that run quite deep.

## My Wonderful Birthday Gift

I speak from personal experience when it comes to the deep roots of iniquity that grieve the Spirit. Allow me to be transparent for a moment and explain.

Before I accepted Christ, I was a tremendously immoral person. As a young man I participated in many behaviors that were defiling and unclean. Then, at the age of nineteen, I married Debbie—a wonderful, pure Christian girl. Not long after that, I was saved, fell in love with God, and began serving Him in ministry.

> On my **BIRTHDAY** the Holy Spirit **ENCOURAGED** me to **ASK** Him for **SOMETHING,** and I did.

Still, I had areas of bondage in my life—areas that Peter called being "bound by iniquity." Even though God blessed me personally and used me to bless others, I still struggled with moral purity.

On the one-year anniversary of my new birth, Debbie said, "Happy birthday! What do you want for your birthday?" I don't recall how I responded to her. But in my quiet time the next morning, I was surprised when I heard the Holy Spirit ask me the same question: *What do you want from Me for your birthday?* After thinking about it, I asked Him for something in my spiritual life that I'd been trying to achieve.

From then on the Lord asked me on my spiritual and natural birthdays. The Holy Spirit encouraged me to ask Him for something, and I did. I didn't ask for material blessings; instead I always asked for something spiritual in nature.

As I neared my thirtieth birthday, I sensed I was also approaching a major milestone in my life. I knew Jesus began His ministry when He was thirty. Although I had already been in Bible college and then full-time ministry for a decade, I hungered to move to a higher level of effectiveness for Him.

The week before my birthday, the Holy Spirit posed that question I'd heard in years past: *Robert, what do you want from Me for your birthday?* I remember that the cry of my heart was to hear the voice of the Lord more clearly. I wanted to know when God was speaking, and I desired to use that hearing heart to help other people. So I asked, "Lord, I would just love to be able to hear You more clearly. That's my birthday request. I want to be able to hear Your voice more fully."

> The **CRY** of my heart was to **HEAR** the voice of the Lord more **CLEARLY**.

My birthday fell on a Monday that year. On the preceding three evenings, I was scheduled to minister at a "prophetic" meeting at a church in another city. Along with a team of others, I would be prophesying over people—giving them words of encouragement and comfort from the Holy Spirit.

On the first night—the Friday before my birthday—I was hearing the voice of the Holy Spirit more clearly than I ever had. I was receiving supernaturally detailed encouragement for others as the Spirit showed me hidden areas of hurt and pain He wanted to heal. I remember thinking, *Wow, I'm already getting my birthday present. I am hearing God so clearly, and I'm already helping people!*

When I went back to my hotel room that night, I was so revved up I couldn't sleep. I turned on the television and began flipping through the channels. Unfortunately, I came across a channel airing a movie no Christian has any business watching. At that moment I needed to turn off the television. The reasons flooded through my mind: *I am a temple of the Holy Spirit, and whatever I give my eyes to, the Holy Spirit sees. And the Holy Spirit is grieved by my sin and iniquity.*

But I didn't. I watched that defiling program. I remember feeling so unclean afterward.

In my quiet time the next morning, I went to God and said, "Lord, I confess this to You. I ask You to forgive me. I don't know why I continue to go back to this part of my life time and again." The truth is that I did know why—it was an unbroken stronghold in my life that carried over from the days before I was saved. I was still bound by iniquity in this area of immorality.

Saturday night I arrived at the church and was expected to minister prophetically again. There was just one problem. I couldn't hear the voice of the Holy Spirit. Nothing. Just silence. I had confessed and repented of my sin. And I knew that God, faithful to His Word, had forgiven me of it. But I still couldn't hear anything. The Holy Spirit was with me, but He was utterly silent. So I just muddled through the best I could. I think it was the longest service I've ever been through.

I was dreading the Sunday morning service. But when I arrived at the church, the senior member of the prophetic team gathered us together and said, "I have a word from the Lord burning in my heart, and I don't think we're supposed to minister prophetically this morning. I think I'm supposed to preach." I tried not to look too relieved.

When the time came, this man got up and said, "The Lord wants me to teach on the subject of iniquity. I want to show you some things in His Word regarding the bondages and strongholds that many of us have—including many mature believers—that hold us back in our effectiveness in God's kingdom."

As I sat in the front row, I thought, *I get it, Lord. This is for me.*

At one point in his message, the speaker began to say that when the Holy Spirit warns us about something and we ignore His warning, it's the equivalent of "stiff-arming" Him. In essence, we tell the Holy Spirit, "I don't want You in my life. I don't want to listen to You. I don't want to follow You—even though You only have my best interests in mind." The speaker then described how we can't stiff-arm the Holy Spirit about sin one moment and then expect Him to speak to us about another matter a few moments later. *Ouch,* I thought.

Then he really brought the point home. He said, "If you've been doing that, you've grieved the Holy Spirit. And God has instructed me to say that if you will humble yourself and come to this altar, He'll set you free."

I remember thinking, *That's me. This whole message was meant for me, and I desperately want to be free. I'm going.*

Yet immediately, I had another thought. *I'm one of the ministers here. I can't go down front and respond to this altar call. I'm not going.*

Then a third thought occurred to me: *People won't assume I have some gross sin in my life. Because I'm a preacher, they'll assume that I haven't been praying and reading my Bible enough. I'm going forward.*

While I was standing there wrestling with myself, the preacher said one more thing: "By the way, I'm not talking about sins like not praying or reading your Bible enough. I'm talking about having a dirty, defiling, shameful sin in your life that has become a stronghold."

Then the Holy Spirit gently said, *Are you still going to go, Robert? Do you still want to be free?*

I answered, "Yes, I'm going. I am going to be the first one down there because I'm tired of living this way."

I walked forward and fell to my knees at that altar. In that moment God did a work of surgery in my heart and life that I still return to this very day. But here's the rest of the story.

Monday morning, as soon as my eyes opened, I heard the clear, sweet voice of the Holy Spirit say two words: *Happy birthday!*

At that moment I realized that I had asked to hear the voice of the Spirit more clearly. But God knew a barrier existed within me—a stronghold of iniquity that repeatedly grieved the Holy Spirit. He knew this sin prevented me from being able to hear Him clearly, so He dealt with it because I asked Him to.

What a wonderful gift. What a wonderful friend.

## SUMMING UP

Has the Holy Spirit spoken something to you through these preceding chapters? Has He shined a light on some dark place in your life? Has He made you aware of some area where you are "bound by iniquity"?

If you'll humble yourself today, He'll set you free.

You can kneel where you are right now and make that place an altar. You can "be the first one down there" as I was. The Holy Spirit will meet you and set you free.

PART 3

# The Grand Entry

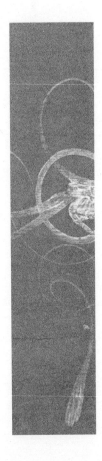

# Wind and Fire

I magine you are talking to a good friend. In the course of the conversation, she tells you about a man you've never heard mentioned before. He sounds interesting, so you ask a few questions.

"Who is he?"

"What is he like?"

"What does he do?"

In essence, we've been posing a similar series of questions about the Holy Spirit. I am introducing you to my best friend by posing and answering some basic questions we would naturally ask about any person.

We began by asking, "Who is this person?" We followed with the important question, "What is this person like?" So let's keep digging deeper into who the Holy Spirit is, by looking at how He empowered the very earliest Christians on the Day of Pentecost.

## DEFINITIONS

Before we look at the Day of Pentecost, we need to examine the word *Pentecostal.* This word carries different meanings for different people. *Pentecostal* has both a cultural definition and a biblical one. The two definitions are quite different from each other.

## Cultural

Let's explore the cultural definition for a moment. To many people in our culture, the term *Pentecostal* describes a person from a very religious tradition where women aren't allowed to wear pants or makeup. Because this tradition also frowns upon women cutting their hair, many of them pile it high on their heads in beehive-like shapes to keep it out of their way. The practice gave rise to an old joke about "the higher the hair, the closer to God."

> **RIGID** prohibitions and practices **CONCERNING DRESS** and **HAIRSTYLES** are little more than **LEGALISTIC** bondage.

In my opinion, rigid prohibitions and practices concerning dress and hairstyles are little more than legalistic bondage. They have little or nothing to do with the Holy Spirit's work within or ministry to God's people. By the way, these "Pentecostal" denominations don't have an exclusive franchise on legalism. Many non-Pentecostal churches are bound by legalism as well.

Still, if that's your definition of the term *Pentecostal,* then I can say with confidence, "No, the Holy Spirit is *not* Pentecostal."

## Biblical

If your definition of *Pentecostal* means "someone who understands and appreciates the historic fulfillment of the Feast of Pentecost as described in Acts 2," then I would answer, "Yes, the Holy Spirit *is* Pentecostal." If the term describes someone who understands that the fruit and gifts and fellowship of the Holy Spirit are all available for us today—and that we all are in desperate need of His empowerment to live the Christian life—then again I would answer, "Yes, the Holy Spirit is Pentecostal!"

So in biblical terms, the quick answer is yes. But if we want to truly understand the answer, we first need to develop an understanding of Pentecost, the event.

## THE DAY OF PENTECOST

To explore why the Day of Pentecost holds such significance for us, let's look to the opening lines of Acts 2:

> When the Day of Pentecost had fully come, they were all with one accord in one place. And suddenly there came a sound from heaven, as of a rushing mighty wind, and it filled the whole house where they were sitting. Then there appeared to them divided tongues, as of fire, and one sat upon each of them. And they were all filled with the Holy Spirit and began to speak with other tongues, as the Spirit gave them utterance. (verses 1–4)

Notice that this passage begins with "they were all with one accord in one place." "They" refers to 120 core followers of Jesus, including the twelve disciples (the twelfth being Matthias, whom they had chosen to replace Judas). This sentence reveals a time, a location, and an attitude. The time is the Jewish feast day of Pentecost. The location described as "in one place" refers to an upper room in Jerusalem. And the attitude of those gathered was "with one accord," meaning they were in unity of heart and mind.

Suddenly, they all heard a tremendous noise that sounded like a gale-force wind. In fact, the sound was so loud that people throughout the city heard it. Even more remarkably, in addition to *hearing* this sound, they *saw* "tongues, as of fire" that appeared to rest upon each of them individually.

After hearing something they'd never heard and seeing something they'd never seen, these people suddenly found themselves with the power to do something they'd never done: "And they were all filled with the Holy Spirit and began to speak with other tongues, as the Spirit gave them utterance" (verse 4).

The Greek word translated "tongues" is *glossa,* which is the root of our English word *glossary.* It means "language." In other words, the 120 people gathered in this room suddenly begin to speak languages they didn't know.

This sequence of events naturally makes us wonder what was occurring. And why did these events happen on this particular day—the Jewish feast day of Pentecost?

## The History of Pentecost

Pentecost was and is one of the three major feasts in the nation of Israel. God Himself instituted these events through Moses. The Jewish holy calendar contains a total of seven such feasts, but all seven fall within three major multiday holidays occurring in the first, third, and seventh months of the Jewish calendar. These three holidays are the Feast of Passover, the Feast of Pentecost, and the Feast of Tabernacles. Until the Roman armies destroyed the Jerusalem temple in AD 70, Jews throughout the Roman world traveled to Jerusalem three times a year to sacrifice and celebrate these feasts.

At the Passover feast they commemorated the event centuries earlier in Egypt when the angel of death passed over the children of Israel on the night before their great deliverance from bondage. On that night they were saved by placing the blood of a lamb upon their doorposts. The event foreshadowed the coming day when all humanity would be offered deliverance from slavery to sin and eternal death through the blood of Jesus, the Lamb of God.

As the name suggests, the Feast of Pentecost was always celebrated on the fiftieth day after the Passover festival. *Pente* is the Greek word for "five," and the suffix *koste* indicates "times ten." This feast commemorated God's giving the Law to Moses on Mount Sinai fifty days after the exodus from Egypt.

As you might know, the number seven appears multiple times throughout Scripture, and it symbolizes completion, full maturity, or perfection. God ordained the Feast of Pentecost to occur seven weeks after Passover, plus one day. Because a week is comprised of seven days, Pentecost comes the day after seven times seven days—a perfectly perfect period of time.

How appropriate this is! For as you are about to see, God ultimately used the divinely ordained Pentecost festival to usher in the person who would make it possible for every believer to become mature and complete.

## What Happened at Pentecost?

First-century Jerusalem was always a busy and crowded place. But during the seasons of the major feasts, Jewish pilgrims from all over the Roman Empire filled the city to overflowing. Two different invasions in the history of Israel and Judah—the first by the Assyrians (722 BC) and the second by the Babylonians (586 BC)—had scattered Jewish people all over the known world. By the time Jesus came onto the scene, more Jews actually lived outside the Roman province that had once been Israel than within it.

Never was Jerusalem more packed with people and from a more diverse range of nations than during the eight-week period leading up to Passover and running through Pentecost. This is the setting for the events of Pentecost Sunday.

We read how the sound of a hurricane filled the room and a visible manifestation of a tongue of fire rested upon each of the 120 individuals present. This resulted in all of them speaking in "other tongues." But what happens next?

> And there were dwelling in Jerusalem Jews, devout men, from every nation under heaven. And when this sound occurred, the multitude came together, and were confused, because everyone heard them speak in his own language. Then they were all amazed and marveled, saying to one another, "Look, are not all these who speak Galileans? And how is it that we hear, each in our own language in which we were born? Parthians and Medes and Elamites, those dwelling in Mesopotamia, Judea and Cappadocia, Pontus and Asia, Phrygia and Pamphylia, Egypt and the parts of Libya adjoining Cyrene, visitors from Rome, both Jews and proselytes, Cretans and Arabs—we hear them speaking in our own tongues the wonderful works of God." So they were all amazed and perplexed, saying to one another, "Whatever could this mean?" Others mocking said, "They are full of new wine." (Acts 2:5–13)

As we mentioned earlier, people far beyond the walls of the upper room heard the sound of the wind. As a result of the sound, a "multitude came together." Once the huge crowd had gathered, they witnessed something that "confused" them. The multitude was bewildered "because everyone heard them speak in his own language."

Two miracles seem to be at work here. First, 120 people suddenly begin speaking in various heavenly languages they'd never before known. Second, thousands of people hear these individuals speaking in their own native languages. In other words, the people from Libya hear them all speaking Libyan. The people from Crete hear the same people speaking Cretan. And the Romans hear the same messages in perfect Latin.

Is it any wonder "they were all amazed and perplexed"? The fact that many of the people speaking were "Galileans" added to the crowd's astonishment. When the refined, city-dwelling Jews in the crowd used the term *Galileans,* they were essentially calling the people uneducated hillbillies. The crowd was saying, "Those country bumpkins from Galilee usually don't speak even one language correctly. How can these hicks suddenly know my language and everyone else's?" What's more, the crowd heard the followers of Jesus "speaking in our own tongues the wonderful works of God" (verse 11).

> Is it any **WONDER** "they were all amazed and **PERPLEXED**"?

Think about how unifying this event must have been. The throng of people gathered was incredibly diverse. They came from different cultures, backgrounds, nations, and languages—all of which separated and isolated them from one another. Yet suddenly, they came together and shared the same experience—the same wonderful message—as one.

This unity, made possible by the Holy Spirit, enabled the first Christians to begin building something of eternal significance. In fact, as Ephesians 2 reminds us, we *are* the building:

Now, therefore, you are no longer strangers and foreigners, but fellow citizens with the saints and members of the

household of God, having been built on the foundation of
the apostles and prophets, Jesus Christ Himself being the chief
cornerstone, in whom the whole building, being fitted together,
grows into a holy temple in the Lord, in whom you also are
being built together for a dwelling place of God in the Spirit.
(verses 19–22)

On the Day of Pentecost, God came down and removed language as a
barrier from knowing Him. By the way, this provides a wonderful preview of
heaven, where every tribe, tongue, and nation gather together, all speaking
one language—the language of praise to God.

This is precisely what happened on the Day of Pentecost.

## What Pentecost Means to Us

Allow me to tell you something about Pentecost that few people grasp. For
the first time since the fall of man in the garden, the coming of the indwelling Holy Spirit empowered people to walk righteously on this earth. We
know that Jesus came to make us righteous *positionally;* in other words, His
death and resurrection put us in right standing with God. But we often miss
the fact that the Holy Spirit empowers us to live in a way consistent with our
righteous position in Christ.

When the Law was given to Israel through Moses, no one could keep it.
The Law gave the Israelites an understanding of what pleased God, but it
couldn't give them the internal ability to live it. With their fallen natures still
intact, they simply had no power to keep the Law.

However, when the Holy Spirit fills a person's life, amazing things hap-
pen. A previously dead human spirit is regenerated by the Holy Spirit. The
Holy Spirit writes a new law upon the heart of that believer. This law isn't the
Ten Commandments; rather, it's the "Law of Love." Anyone who fulfills this
law will never be guilty of violating the Ten Commandments or displeasing
God in any way. In fact, Jesus said the entire teaching of the Law and the
Prophets could be summed up with, "Love God with all your heart," and,
"Love your neighbor as yourself."

But that's not all. When a person receives a full release of the Holy Spirit's power, he receives the empowerment to walk in love. In other words, you can't walk righteously without the power of the Holy Spirit.

> You can't **WALK** righteously **WITHOUT** the **POWER** of the Holy Spirit.

This is what the apostle Paul proclaims throughout Romans 8, beginning with the familiar and wonderful promise: "There is therefore now no condemnation to those who are in Christ Jesus" (verse 1). Whenever we see the word *therefore* in Scripture, we should look for what preceded that promise. In this case, we can look back at Romans 7 where Paul expresses thoughts that every frustrated believer can identify with:

> For I have the desire to do what is good, but I cannot carry it out. For what I do is not the good I want to do; no, the evil I do not want to do—this I keep on doing....
>
> What a wretched man I am! Who will rescue me from this body of death? (verses 18–19, 24, NIV)

Of course, when Paul wrote his letter to the Romans, no chapter divisions existed. He went right from this pitiful heart cry for holiness ("Wretched man.... Who will rescue me?") to the solution. Paul reminds us that we are righteous *positionally* and then goes on to describe the key to living in a way that is consistent with our position:

> There is therefore now no condemnation to those who are in Christ Jesus, who do not walk according to the flesh, but according to the Spirit. (Romans 8:1)

Paul continues by explaining the difference between living in accordance with our old "flesh" natures and living in the Spirit: "For those who live according to the flesh set their minds on the things of the flesh, but those who live according to the Spirit, the things of the Spirit" (verse 5).

Again and again, Paul emphasizes the role of the Holy Spirit in enabling and empowering us to live lives that are in line with the righteous position Jesus purchased for us through His blood:

> For if you live according to the flesh you will die; but if by the Spirit you put to death the deeds of the body, you will live. For as many as are led by the Spirit of God, these are sons of God. For you did not receive the spirit of bondage again to fear, but you received the Spirit of adoption by whom we cry out, "Abba, Father." The Spirit Himself bears witness with our spirit that we are children of God, and if children, then heirs—heirs of God and joint heirs with Christ, if indeed we suffer with Him, that we may also be glorified together. (verses 13–17)

As these verses make clear, when we cultivate a friendship with the Holy Spirit and yield ourselves to His influence, we can cease feeling like wretched people. Only then can we stop doing the bad things we don't want to do and succeed at doing the good things we want to do.

## The Holy Spirit Changes Everything

For the twelve disciples of Jesus and the 108 others gathered in the room on Pentecost Sunday, the outpouring of the Holy Spirit changed everything.

Before that day they struggled to understand the Scriptures. Afterward they realized that the entire Old Testament pointed prophetically and symbolically to the life and redeeming work of Jesus. What had previously been shrouded in mystery suddenly became completely clear.

Before that day the disciples were timid and afraid—hiding in locked rooms and dreading the knock at the door. A little girl had intimidated Peter, the burly fisherman, into swearing and denying he even knew Jesus. After that remarkable day, the disciples personified boldness and confidence. They proclaimed Jesus in public squares and synagogues. When arrested and threatened with beatings or worse if they didn't stop preaching, they shrugged and said, "No can do." They no longer feared the disapproval of man!

The transformation brought by the outpouring of the Holy Spirit on the Day of Pentecost was nothing short of astonishing. That brings us to the next logical questions: Can we experience the miracle of Pentecost Sunday still today? And if so, how?

# Pentecost Now

I f you are like me, you occasionally envy the people in the Bible who witnessed extraordinary works of God or spectacular signs and wonders. You and I cannot witness the parting of the Red Sea, nor can we be a part of Noah's amazing feat of construction (that ship has sailed, so to speak). But I can assure you of one thing: even though Pentecost, that amazing day, is two thousand years in the past, you and I *can still* experience it!

## EACH AND ALL

To explore the reasons why we can experience Pentecost now, let's return to Acts 2:3–4:

> Then there appeared to them divided tongues, as of fire, and one sat upon *each* of them. And they were *all* filled with the Holy Spirit and began to speak with other tongues, as the Spirit gave them utterance.

I've emphasized *each* and *all* in these verses because these words tell us something important about what happened that day. The 120 individuals in that room represented a wide spectrum of society. Rich and influential people like Joseph of Arimathea and Nicodemus were probably there. In addition, the formerly blind beggars and lepers whom Jesus had healed, and former prostitutes He had ministered to, were surely there too. Some, like the twelve disciples, were in "full-time ministry." Others were simple merchants, farmers, or homemakers.

You'll recall that a tongue of flame signifying the indwelling presence of the outpoured Holy Spirit came and rested upon each of them. If you and I had been in that room, you would have seen a tongue of flame above my head and I would have seen one above your head! In other words, this baptism in the Spirit of God wasn't only for the elite or those in full-time ministry. They were "all filled with the Holy Spirit," and they all "began to speak with other tongues, as the Spirit gave them utterance."

The baptism in the Holy Spirit is for everyone. Again, if we had been present on the Day of Pentecost, I suspect we wouldn't have been able to see our own flames. Why? Because I think you would have to receive and believe *by faith* that God had given you a tongue of flame also. You would need to trust that not just the "spiritual people" were empowered; everyone was.

Allow me to let you in on a secret. That's exactly what you must do to receive the Holy Spirit. You receive Him and His ministry the same way you received Jesus—by faith.

## The Future and Afar

So, can we experience the Holy Spirit's power today? For an answer, let's back up another step and look at some important words of Jesus in the previous chapter of Acts:

> And being assembled together with them, He commanded them not to depart from Jerusalem, but to wait for the Promise of the Father, "which," He said, "you have heard from Me; for John truly baptized with water, but you shall be baptized with the Holy Spirit not many days from now." (Acts 1:4–5)

Notice the word "Promise" in Jesus's statement: "the Promise of the Father." This promise isn't a *what* but a *who:* "For John truly baptized with water, but you shall be baptized with the Holy Spirit not many days from now."

Keeping in mind Jesus's description of the Holy Spirit as a promise, look at what happened in the immediate aftermath of the Holy Spirit's outpouring on Pentecost Sunday. After the sound and commotion draws a huge crowd in the area of Jerusalem where the 120 are gathered, the people are "all amazed and perplexed, saying to one another, 'Whatever could this mean?'" (Acts 2:12).

In response Peter stands up and delivers the first Holy Spirit–inspired prophetic sermon ever delivered. Off the cuff, he cites Old Testament passages that spoke of the outpouring of the Holy Spirit and how His coming would empower God's people to prophesy. The formerly timid Peter finishes by boldly proclaiming Jesus as the Messiah.

> These **PEOPLE** had **WITNESSED** a supernatural **DEMONSTRATION** of the Holy Spirit's **POWER**.

In support of Peter's preaching, the Holy Spirit does what He was specifically sent to do: He convicts hearts and draws people to Jesus. Notice how the people listening to Peter respond:

> Now when they heard this, they were cut to the heart, and said to Peter and the rest of the apostles, "Men and brethren, what shall we do?" (Acts 2:37)

These people had witnessed a supernatural demonstration of the Holy Spirit's power and heard a sermon about how the outpouring of the Holy Spirit was prophesied by the prophet Joel. With their question they were essentially asking, "What do we need to do to have a relationship with God like you have?" Of course, Peter happily answers their question:

> Repent, and let every one of you be baptized in the name of Jesus Christ for the remission of sins; and you shall receive the gift of the Holy Spirit. For the promise is to you and to your children, and to all who are afar off, as many as the Lord our God will call. (verses 38–39)

Peter quickly outlines three simple steps:

1. Repent.
2. Be water baptized.
3. Receive the Holy Spirit.

What Peter outlines here goes two steps beyond simply receiving salvation. He presents a road map for experiencing every wonderful thing that is available to the believer in Christ.

Notice that Peter ends his answer by referring to "the promise." Of course, just ten days earlier, Jesus had referred to the Holy Spirit as the promise. Now Peter says that the promise belongs "to you and to your children, and to all who are afar off, as many as the Lord our God will call."

Peter makes it clear that the promise of the Holy Spirit belongs not only to the people he's speaking directly to but to future generations as well ("your children"). And the phrase "all who are afar off" refers directly to Robert Morris in north Texas. And it also refers directly to you. The promise belongs to anyone God calls—in any place and in any time.

## More than a One-Time Event

Has God called you? Yes, He has. Can you experience Pentecost? Oh yes— it's a promise.

However, some skeptics argue that the promise can't hold now because Pentecost was a one-time event. However, Pentecost wasn't even a one-time event in the book of Acts. Other groups of people receive an outpouring of the Holy Spirit in Acts 8, 10, and 19 too.

In Acts 8, the apostles send Peter and John to minister to a group of new Christians in Samaria:

> When the apostles in Jerusalem heard that Samaria had accepted the word of God, they sent Peter and John to them. When they arrived, they prayed for them that they might receive the Holy Spirit, because the Holy Spirit had not yet come upon any of them; they had simply been baptized into the name of the Lord Jesus. Then Peter and John

placed their hands on them, and they received the Holy Spirit. (verses 14–17, NIV)

In Acts 10, Peter travels to a group of Gentiles in Caesarea who are hungry to hear about Jesus. Up to this point, only Jews had been saved and received the Holy Spirit. As Peter tells this eager group the basics of the gospel story, "the Holy Spirit came on all who heard the message. The circumcised believers who had come with Peter were astonished that the gift of the Holy Spirit had been poured out even on the Gentiles. For they heard them speaking in tongues and praising God" (Acts 10:44–46, NIV).

> Some **SKEPTICS** argue that the **PROMISE** can't hold **NOW** because Pentecost was a **ONE-TIME** event.

And in Acts 19, "when Paul placed his hands on them, the Holy Spirit came on them, and they spoke in tongues and prophesied" (verse 6, NIV).

I've heard some people say, "I can't experience Pentecost because it happened two thousand years ago." My response is to pose a question: Can you be saved because of Jesus's death and resurrection? Of course! Every day people come to salvation by placing their faith in Jesus Christ. Well, that happened two thousand years ago too. You weren't alive when Jesus was on this earth, and yet salvation is fully available to you now, because through His death and victory over the grave, Jesus opened the door once and for always.

The same holds true with the Holy Spirit. Pentecost was the initial outpouring of the Holy Spirit, initiating an experience that continues to this very day. The Holy Spirit is still here, still working, still drawing people to Jesus, and still filling them with power from on high.

We *can* receive Jesus as Savior. We *need* to do so. It's vitally important. We *can* receive a baptism in the Holy Spirit. We *need* to do that as well. It, too, is vitally important. A brief examination of the feasts of Israel reveals why.

## What Israel's Feasts Mean to Us

Passover. Pentecost. Tabernacles. As we observed earlier, God established these three major feasts in the Old Testament. They are sometimes called the pilgrimage festivals because the entire Jewish nation assembled in Jerusalem to worship and sacrifice at the temple. While we've explored the historical connection between the Feast of Pentecost and the Day of Pentecost, let's look briefly at the other two feasts and their significance for us today.

### Passover

Passover involved the sacrifice of a lamb whose shed blood would atone for the sins of the nation. While this feast was clearly fulfilled in Jesus's death on the cross, you might not be aware of how many amazing parallels actually exist. For example, the Passover lamb was killed at 9:00 a.m. by the cutting of its throat. At 9:00 a.m. on the day of Jesus's crucifixion, they nailed the spikes into His hands and feet. At 3:00 p.m. the Passover lamb was put in a stone oven for roasting in preparation for the Passover meal. At 3:00 p.m. the day Jesus died, He was put in a stone tomb.

After the Friday Passover lamb was placed in the oven, the father of the Jewish household took a loaf of unleavened bread and hid it somewhere in the house. Leaven or yeast represented sin, so the unleavened loaf symbolized purity and sinlessness. On Sunday, the day after the Sabbath, the father retrieved the hidden bread and held it up to God, waving it before Him as a "firstfruits" offering of the harvest. God the Father hid the body of His sinless Son in the tomb. On Sunday Jesus emerged as "the firstborn among many brethren" (Romans 8:29) and "the firstfruits of those who have fallen asleep" (1 Corinthians 15:20).

### Tabernacles

So what about the third great pilgrimage feast—the Feast of Tabernacles? Actually, it has not yet been fulfilled. The Feast of Tabernacles has another name, the Feast of Trumpets.

The Passover feast was fulfilled in a single day. Likewise, the initial Pentecost was fulfilled in a single day. In the same way, a day is coming—the

Bible says no man knows the day or the hour—when a trumpet will sound and Jesus will return for His bride. Then all Christians will forever "tabernacle" with the Lord. This future day when Christ returns will fulfill the Feast of Tabernacles. That will be a good day!

## SOME PERSONAL QUESTIONS

Can you personally experience the fulfillment of Passover, which means being forgiven of your sins by accepting Jesus Christ as your Savior? Of course you can.

As a believer, can you personally experience the fulfillment of Tabernacles, which means going to heaven and being with the Lord on some future day? Again, the answer is yes.

If you are a Christian, you have already personally experienced what the Feast of Passover represented. And one day we'll experience what the Feast of Tabernacles represented. So that presents an obvious question about the feast I skipped.

Doesn't it stand to reason that we can also personally experience what the Feast of Pentecost represented? If we can know the fulfilled realities of Passover and Tabernacles, we can surely know the fulfilled reality of Pentecost.

So do you? Have you experienced what numerous groups of believers in the book of Acts experienced? Or let me ask this question as Paul does in Acts 19: "Did you receive the Holy Spirit when you believed?" (verse 2).

## THE START OF MY FRIENDSHIP WITH THE HOLY SPIRIT

It took me a while to answer this question for myself. I'd been a born-again Christian for several years before I experienced the fulfillment of Pentecost. A pastor who had been filled with the Holy Spirit opened my eyes to the need to receive the fullness of the Holy Spirit. He was preaching and gave an invitation at the end of his sermon. With some trepidation and misgivings, I went forward. Keep in mind, I'd received a lot of negative teaching about the Holy Spirit in the past and I'd seen some pretty odd people who claimed to be walking advertisements for Him.

I remember thinking, *Okay, Holy Spirit. I want to receive You. But I don't want to change my hair, I don't want to be weird, and I definitely don't want to speak in tongues.* I didn't use these exact words, but the attitude of my heart said, *Holy Spirit, I want You to come in, but only on my terms and conditions. I'm receiving You, even though I have some reservations about it. I want You to know that I have some concerns and stipulations, but if You can work around my conditions and promise to behave Yourself, then You're welcome in my life. Kind of...I guess.*

Not surprisingly, I didn't see much increase in power or miraculous activity in my life following that weak and insulting invitation. About a year later, after spending some serious time studying what Scripture says regarding the work and ministry of the Holy Spirit, I became deeply convicted and repentant about my former attitude. I realized I'd allowed my religious prejudice and false conceptions to bind me from fully receiving the Holy Spirit.

Not long afterward, I again went forward during an altar call, but this time I had an open and willing heart that said, *God, I trust You, and I want everything You have for me. I want to be the most effective servant of Yours I can possibly be. I want to be empowered the same way the disciples were in the upper room. I want Your gifts. I want Your empowerment. I want You, Holy Spirit of God.*

> God, I **TRUST** You and I **WANT** everything **YOU** have for **ME**.

That's when I really received the Holy Spirit.

A lot of people have a similar experience with the Holy Spirit. They go through some motions. They pray a prayer. But their hearts are saying, *I want some of what You're offering, Holy Spirit, but not all of it. I want to pick and choose among the gifts You want to bring me because I don't trust You enough to choose for me.*

However, God doesn't operate on those terms. Trusting in His goodness and surrendering to His plans and purposes are the keys to life and blessing in His kingdom.

## Summing Up

I wrote this book not for informational purposes but for transformational purposes. My goal isn't to satisfy your curiosity or to add to your wealth of knowledge. My goal is to stimulate your hunger for God. I want you to be transformed by His Word.

So, may I ask you a personal question? Do you need to receive the Holy Spirit? Do you need to experience the fulfilled reality of Pentecost? Before you answer, perhaps you should ask *Him* that question with an open heart of trust and humility.

If the answer is yes, all you need to do is ask. But you must ask without conditions. Why? Because He is God. Just remember that He isn't a weird God. He is also not a harsh God. He is a kind and gentle God who desires to fill us with love, peace, and joy! Open your heart to Him, and don't allow any abuses or misuses that you've seen in the past to cause you to ask in fear.

In the same way that you received Jesus by faith, open up your heart and receive the Holy Spirit with faith and joy!

PART 4

# The Power Transfer

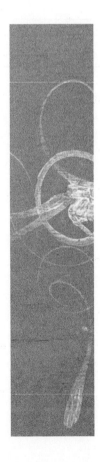

# Immersed

Y ou've probably seen photos of the Leaning Tower of Pisa in Italy. This tower is actually the bell tower of the city of Pisa's cathedral. Did you realize that this famous landmark was meant to stand vertically? But because of a poorly designed foundation, the tower began leaning soon after construction started in 1173.

Foundations are important, because they transfer the weight of a building into the ground itself. Think about the foundation of your home. It might be a concrete slab, piers and beams to "float" most of your home above the ground and potential floodwaters, or a block or poured basement foundation. On large buildings the foundations often extend all the way to a bedrock level in the earth.

We've been learning that the Holy Spirit is a person who can be your friend. We understand now that He's not a mystical or impersonal force but a person you can know and love and trust. This foundation is vital to approaching the next subject with a proper orientation.

## THE DEVIL STIRS UP CONTROVERSY

"Baptism *in* the Holy Spirit."

"The baptism *of* the Holy Spirit."

Have you heard either of these terms used in Christian circles? If you have, those mentions likely came with some controversy or negativity attached to them.

We shouldn't be surprised that the devil wants to stir up as much controversy as possible around the ministry and methods of the third person of the Trinity. Seeing God's people walking in close friendship with the Holy Spirit and being empowered by that fellowship is Satan's worst nightmare. It would mean hundreds of millions of little Jesuses undoing all of the devil's hard work. In fact, Acts 10:38 tells us "how God anointed Jesus of Nazareth with the Holy Spirit and with power, who went about doing good and healing all who were oppressed by the devil."

Why does so much confusion surround the connection between baptism and the Holy Spirit? It comes in part because the Bible mentions several different baptisms, two of which involve the Holy Spirit.

Most of us are familiar with water baptism. We can easily deal with this baptism because the Bible depicts it clearly—take John the Baptist's activity in the Jordan River, for example. And if you attend a church that practices it, you see it with your own eyes all the time.

Still, the Bible mentions two baptisms that you can't see with your physical eyes. You can only see the aftereffects of them in a person's life. Let's explore all three to understand the differences.

## BAPTISM OF THE HOLY SPIRIT

The first of the baptisms a person can and should experience is mentioned in 1 Corinthians 12:13: "For by one Spirit we were all baptized into one body— whether Jews or Greeks, whether slaves or free."

Note the grammar in this verse. (Please don't let your eyes glaze over because I mentioned the word *grammar* and am about to point out some of those parts of speech you studied in ninth grade. This is good stuff, and it will help you.) Do you see the preposition *by* at the beginning of the verse? The dictionary tells us that *by* means "through the agency or instrumentality of." In other words, *by* refers to who is doing the *doing*.

So, who is doing the baptizing in this verse? The Holy Spirit. When you and I experienced salvation, we were both baptized into the same body—the body of Christ. And the Holy Spirit is the agent who did the baptizing. This is the baptism *of* the Holy Spirit. But it's not the baptism *in* the Holy Spirit.

If you've been born again, it's only because the Holy Spirit drew you, wooed you, convicted you of your sinful state, and made you aware of your separation from God. When you responded to that wooing by choosing Jesus, the Holy Spirit did a supernatural work of regeneration in your spirit, making you spiritually alive—now and for eternity. At that moment you became a part of something much bigger than yourself. You became a member of the body of Christ. As Paul reminds us in Romans 12:4–5:

> Just as each of us has one body with many members, and these
> members do not all have the same function, so in Christ we who are
> many form one body, and each member belongs to all the others. (NIV)

## WATER BAPTISM

The way you became a "member" of the body of Christ is by the Holy Spirit "baptizing" you into it. Then, if we are obedient to the commands of Scripture, we choose to experience a second baptism, this one in water. As I mentioned before, confusion about this baptism is less an issue because we see it happening with our natural eyes and we see exactly who does the baptizing. This type of baptism is what Jesus had in mind when He said, "Go therefore and make disciples of all the nations, baptizing them in the name of the Father and of the Son and of the Holy Spirit" (Matthew 28:19).

These first two baptisms aren't all that controversial. Of course, you can always find some religious person ready to argue over one point or another regarding salvation and water baptism and exactly *what* spiritually happens exactly *when*. Still, there's broad agreement and understanding that when we are born again, the Holy Spirit baptizes us into the body of Christ, and that water baptism is an outward sign of what has happened inwardly.

As Ephesians 2:1 reminds us, we "were dead in trespasses and sins" before we came to Jesus. And we bury dead people. But a few verses later, Paul describes the miracle of salvation this way:

Even when we were dead in trespasses, [God] made us alive
together with Christ (by grace you have been saved), and raised
us up together, and made us sit together in the heavenly places
in Christ Jesus. (verses 5–6)

Dead. Buried. Raised to new life. This is the wonderful symbolism of
water baptism.

## Baptism in the Holy Spirit

I mentioned earlier that the best-known baptizer in Scripture was John the
Baptist. Because he is even described as the baptizer, we should pay close attention when he says something about baptism—particularly when he mentions a type of baptism other than water. In Matthew 3:11 he says,

I indeed baptize you with water unto repentance, but He who
is coming after me is mightier than I, whose sandals I am not
worthy to carry. He will baptize you with the Holy Spirit
and fire.

Nearly everyone knows and agrees that John is talking about Jesus. So,
allow me to paraphrase John's statement: "You've seen me immersing repentant people in water, but I am just a forerunner for the much greater One,
Jesus, who will immerse reborn people in the fire of the Holy Spirit."

John's statement is one of just a handful of statements or accounts
present in all four gospels—Matthew, Mark, Luke, and John. Each of the
gospels tells the story of Jesus from a different perspective, emphasizing a
different aspect of Jesus's ministry and for different audiences. So we
shouldn't be surprised that very few stories or statements appear in all four
books. But this statement does. Let's have a quick look at the other three.

I indeed baptized you with water, but He will baptize you with the
Holy Spirit. (Mark 1:8)

John answered them all, "I baptize you with water. But one more
powerful than I will come, the thongs of whose sandals I am not
worthy to untie. He will baptize you with the Holy Spirit and with
fire." (Luke 3:16, NIV)

I did not know Him, but He who sent me to baptize with water said
to me, "Upon whom you see the Spirit descending, and remaining on
Him, this is He who baptizes with the Holy Spirit." (John 1:33)

You'll find accounts of the death and the resurrection of Jesus in all four
gospels. They are obviously central to the gospel story and explain vital
truths believers need to understand. So, I believe it's significant that the baptism in the Holy Spirit is in all four as well.

Here are some simple, easy-to-answer questions about the four verses we
just read.

*Who is doing the baptism in these verses?* It's Jesus!

*What is He baptizing us in or with?* The Holy Spirit! In other words, only
Jesus performs this baptism, immersing us in the Holy Spirit. Scripture
clearly tells us this four times, in four separate gospels.

To compare, let's look back at that baptism of salvation Paul describes in
1 Corinthians 12:13: "For by one Spirit we were all baptized into one body—
whether Jews or Greeks, whether slaves or free." The baptizer in this case is
the Holy Spirit, baptizing us into Jesus. In the Gospels we see the reverse. We
see a baptism where Jesus is the baptizer, baptizing us into the Holy Spirit.

These cannot possibly refer to the same baptism. Yet many Christians
hold tightly to a theology that says these two baptisms are the same event.
They think that just two baptisms exist: the spiritual one of being baptized
*by* the Holy Spirit *into* the body of Christ, and the physical symbolic one
where a pastor immerses them in water. But this is incorrect.

It should really be apparent that beyond the baptism into Jesus (the new
birth) and water baptism, Scripture repeatedly describes this third baptism
where Jesus baptizes us into the Holy Spirit. Jesus even commanded His
disciples to wait in Jerusalem until they received it.

How could Jesus baptizing us in the Holy Spirit possibly be a bad thing—especially when it's so plainly present in the Bible? First, Jesus—the One who loved us so much He died for us—is doing the baptizing. Second, the third member of the Trinity—God the Holy Spirit—is whom we are being immersed into! Yet countless Christians avoid this experience as if it is a horrible or hurtful thing.

Only Satan could get so many people's thinking so upside down.

## AN EXTRAORDINARY PRIVILEGE

Having the empowering, enabling, and energizing presence of the Holy Spirit as a constant companion and friend is an extraordinary privilege only New Covenant believers can enjoy. The greatest of the Old Testament saints would have marveled at the blessing we've been given. They would shake their heads in utter disbelief that so many of God's people turn their noses up at the opportunity.

Remember John 1:33 above? There, John the Baptist says God told him, "Upon whom you see the Spirit descending, and remaining on Him, this is He who baptizes with the Holy Spirit."

This verse brings us an important insight into the ministry of the Holy Spirit before and after the outpouring on the Day of Pentecost. Note the words "descending" and "remaining" in the verse. Throughout the Old Testament, we find many instances where the Holy Spirit would descend upon someone, but He did not remain. Prophets, judges, warriors, and kings all experienced short seasons where the Holy Spirit's power and enabling came upon them. But it only lasted for a season.

Immediately after Jesus's water baptism, He became the first person in history to have the Holy Spirit both *descend* and *remain* upon Him. On the Day of Pentecost, the Holy Spirit descended upon the 120 gathered and remained upon them for the rest of their lives. The same thing is available to you and me. As a matter of fact, I've experienced it. Once I got over all my suspicions, hang-ups, and distorted preconceptions, I threw my heart open to the ministry of the Holy Spirit and asked Jesus to baptize me in Him. And the Holy Spirit descended upon me and has remained with me since. My Christian life has never been the same!

## A FINAL QUESTION

I ask you to ponder one more question: what were Jesus's final instructions to His disciples?

Jesus appeared to His disciples off and on for forty days following the Resurrection. Finally, a day came when He gave them words of instruction for the last time. This took place right before His ascension into heaven. Many people think His final words of instruction are found in the final two verses of the book of Matthew:

> "Go therefore and make disciples of all the nations, baptizing them
> in the name of the Father and of the Son and of the Holy Spirit,
> teaching them to observe all things that I have commanded you;
> and lo, I am with you always, even to the end of the age." Amen.
> (Matthew 28:19–20)

That certainly does sound final—especially with an "Amen" at the end. However, these words were not the last Jesus spoke to His disciples. Jesus's final word of instruction to His followers was not "go." It was "wait." We find this command recorded in the final chapter of Luke. Jesus appears to His disciples and gives them some words of explanation and instruction. When He finishes speaking, they see Him taken up into the heavens. Right before that moment He says, "Behold, I send the Promise of My Father upon you; but tarry in the city of Jerusalem until you are endued with power from on high" (Luke 24:49).

> Jesus's **FINAL** word of **INSTRUCTION** to His followers was not "go." It was **"WAIT."**

The word *tarry* simply means "wait." Don't you think Jesus would very carefully choose the words He knew would be the last the disciples would hear Him speak? Wouldn't you assume these are important instructions?

His final instruction was to wait. Wait for what? The Promise. As we learned earlier, Jesus's last words are also recorded in the first chapter of Acts:

> And being assembled together with them, He commanded them not to depart from Jerusalem, but to *wait for the Promise* of the Father, "which," He said, "you have heard from Me; for John truly baptized with water, but *you shall be baptized with the Holy Spirit* not many days from now." (verses 4–5)

We previously saw that each of the four gospels records a promise that Jesus will baptize His followers in the Holy Spirit. Now we have a fifth mention of baptism in the Holy Spirit.

Jesus told His disciples to "wait" before they "go" change the world. He knew that if they went without the empowerment of the Holy Spirit, nothing would happen. He was telling them, "Don't try to do anything I've instructed and called you to do until you've received this additional baptism. You'll only be striving in your own natural ability, and nothing of lasting spiritual value will be accomplished. Wait! Wait for what I promised you—a helper."

If you've been born again, the Holy Spirit baptized you into Jesus at the moment you were saved. But let me ask you, have you asked Jesus to baptize you into the Holy Spirit? If not, in whose power are you attempting to live the Christian life?

# Three Baptisms,
# Three Witnesses

I remember hearing a lot about the great evangelist D. L. Moody back when I was in Bible school. I consistently heard quotes and anecdotes about Moody from my professors. Interestingly, the official position of my school was that the power of the Holy Spirit was only for first-century Christians. We learned that the Holy Spirit stopped baptizing people back in the days of Peter and Paul. Yet Moody was consistently held up before students as a shining example of an effective preacher and evangelist. And rightly so.

Imagine my surprise years later when I finally read Moody's autobiography and learned that he'd had a transformative experience with the Holy Spirit years after he was saved and went into the ministry.

In the late 1800s, Moody was the pastor of a church in Chicago, which met in a rented room. He thought he was doing pretty well in ministry. But eventually two elderly Free Methodist women in his congregation—Auntie Cook and Mrs. Snow—began to pray for Moody to receive the baptism in the Holy Spirit. When these prayer warriors told him what they'd been asking God to do in his life, he thanked them for their prayers but tactfully explained that he'd received all the Holy Spirit there was to get when he was saved.

According to Moody, as these women tenaciously continued to pray for him, he began to realize that he didn't have much in the way of supernatural power operating in his ministry—at least not the kind he saw flowing through the ordinary Christians found in his Bible. In Acts 2 he saw clearly that an outpouring of the Holy Spirit upon a person was what imparted the power to be a witness for Jesus. He ultimately came to the conclusion that he indeed lacked another baptism. He began praying for it, and he also asked the two women if they would pray with him to receive an outpouring of God's power. Not long afterward, God answered the cry of D. L. Moody's heart.

Moody had been invited to preach in England. For a few days before his ship was scheduled to depart, he was in New York City. One day he was taking a walk when something remarkable happened. As his friend R. A. Torrey described it years later,

> He was walking up Wall Street in New York…and in the midst of the bustle and hurry of that city his prayer was answered; the power of God fell upon him as he walked up the street and he had to hurry off to the house of a friend and ask that he might have a room by himself, and in that room he stayed alone for hours; and the Holy Ghost came upon him filling his soul with such joy that at last he had to ask God to withhold His hand, lest he die on the spot from very joy. He went out from that place with the power of the Holy Ghost upon him, and when he got to London, the power of God wrought through him mightily in North London and hundreds were added to the churches.*

## Not as Hard as It Seems

If even the great evangelist D. L. Moody struggled with the reality of multiple baptisms that the Bible teaches about, it's not surprising that many Christians struggle with the same truth. Perhaps you're still processing this whole concept. If so, it might surprise you even more to learn that God considers this teaching to be "elementary." That's the message of this passage:

---

* R. A. Torrey, *Why God Used D. L. Moody* (Chicago: Fleming H. Revell, 1923), 53–54.

Therefore, leaving the discussion of the elementary principles of Christ, let us go on to perfection, not laying again the foundation of repentance from dead works and of faith toward God, of the doctrine of baptisms, of laying on of hands, of resurrection of the dead, and of eternal judgment. (Hebrews 6:1–2)

Here the writer of Hebrews says he would like to move on from the grade-school instruction and start teaching his readers meatier and deeper things. He considers things such as "repentance from dead works," "faith toward God," and other principles as foundational. One of those foundational teachings is "the doctrine of baptisms" (plural).

So, I wonder if our religious traditions have made the topic of baptisms harder than it needs to be. Throughout more than twenty-five years of ministry, I've realized that many Christians need help seeing that Scripture indeed teaches about three separate and distinct baptisms. With that in mind, I'd like to give you several biblical examples of all three baptisms. As the writer of Hebrews notes, we can't go on to maturity unless we have a solid understanding of this "elementary" truth.

## Peter's Pentecost Sermon

Let's expand on a passage we've already discussed. You'll recall that Peter delivers a sermon immediately after the outpouring of the Holy Spirit on the Day of Pentecost (see Acts 2). In response to Peter's preaching, a number of his Jewish listeners fall under the conviction of the Holy Spirit. Acts 2:37 tells us, "Now when they heard this, they were cut to the heart, and said to Peter and the rest of the apostles, 'Men and brethren, what shall we do?'"

"What shall we do?" That's a pretty broad question—certainly far more general than the question asked by the Philippian jailer after an earthquake frees Paul and Silas in Acts 16: "Sirs, what must I do to be saved?" (verse 30). The jailer asks only about the first baptism—salvation—so Paul's answer only addresses that issue: "Believe on the Lord Jesus Christ, and you will be saved" (verse 31). How does Peter respond to this more generic question?

Then Peter said to them, "Repent, and let every one of you be baptized in the name of Jesus Christ for the remission of sins; and you shall receive the gift of the Holy Spirit. For the promise is to you and to your children, and to all who are afar off, as many as the Lord our God will call." (Acts 2:38–39)

Notice that in the active verbs in these verses, Peter outlines all three baptisms. He says,

1. *Repent.* This is the vital primary step in the baptism of salvation.
2. *Be baptized.* Peter urges his listeners to follow Jesus's example in water baptism.
3. *Receive the gift of the Holy Spirit.* This is the third baptism. As Peter indicates here, the Holy Spirit will not force Himself upon anyone. He must be "received."

## GREAT JOY IN SAMARIA

The recounting of the Day of Pentecost in Acts 2 isn't the only place we see all three baptisms outlined. In Acts 8 we find the evangelist Philip preaching and teaching in Samaria. After a revival breaks out, many people are healed, delivered from demonic oppression, and saved. Then, verse 12 tells us, "But when they believed Philip as he preached the things concerning the kingdom of God and the name of Jesus Christ, both men and women were baptized."

Two of the three baptisms are found in this verse. "They believed" means the people received the baptism of salvation. Then they were baptized in water. That's two. What about the third baptism—immersion in the Holy Spirit? Let's keep reading:

Now when the apostles who were at Jerusalem heard that Samaria had received the word of God, they sent Peter and John to them, who, when they had come down, prayed for them that they might receive the Holy Spirit. For as yet He had fallen upon none of them. They had only been baptized in the name of the Lord Jesus. (verses 14–16)

Notice what this passage *doesn't* say. It doesn't tell us that when the apostles in Jerusalem heard that Samaria had received the Word of God, they sent Peter and John who gave them the right hand of Christian fellowship *because they had everything they needed.*

In the early years of my Christian walk, this is precisely what I was taught. I was told that once I was saved and water baptized, I had everything I needed to live the Christian life. Of course, now I know that without receiving the Holy Spirit, I was living a powerless and defeated life of minimal effectiveness in God's kingdom.

> Without **RECEIVING** the Holy Spirit, I was **LIVING** a **POWERLESS** and defeated life of **MINIMAL** effectiveness in God's **KINGDOM**.

Peter and John don't dare do that kind of disservice to the new believers of Samaria. They are happy that these folks had received the first two baptisms. But the first thing the disciples ask is whether or not the new believers had received the third one. When the answer comes back no, the apostles immediately address that situation: "Then they laid hands on them, and they received the Holy Spirit" (verse 17).

Then, and only then, were these new Christians fully equipped to be all God called them to be.

By the way, note that this scene doesn't take place in Acts 2. I've heard people argue that being baptized in the Holy Spirit only occurred on the Day of Pentecost. Yet these events in Samaria occurred months or even years after those of Acts 2. And even this isn't the last time we'll see people experiencing three baptisms.

## THE PATTERN CONTINUES IN EPHESUS

In Acts 19, many years after the Pentecost outpouring, we hear about the apostle Paul's ministry in Ephesus:

> And it happened, while Apollos was at Corinth, that Paul, having passed through the upper regions, came to Ephesus. And finding

some *disciples* he said to them, "Did you receive the Holy Spirit when you *believed*?" (verses 1–2)

Interestingly, the people Paul encounters are "disciples" who already "believed," meaning they are followers of Jesus Christ. Now notice Paul's question. "Did you receive the Holy Spirit when you believed?" Paul doesn't seem to have any doubt in his mind that someone can come to saving faith in Jesus Christ yet not receive the fullness of the Holy Spirit. In other words, Paul knows that a person can be baptized by the Spirit into Christ (salvation), yet not be baptized by Jesus into the Holy Spirit.

I can recall studying Acts in Sunday school when I was a boy, but I don't remember reading these two verses. I now wonder how many teachers and preachers skip over these verses rather than face being confronted with their plain-as-the-nose-on-your-face message. This question is in your Bible: "Did you receive the Holy Spirit when you believed?"

By the way, I love the response of the believers: "We have not so much as heard whether there is a Holy Spirit" (verse 2).

Maybe these people went to the same church I attended as a boy! Someone told them enough about Jesus so they could be saved. But they haven't even heard of the Holy Spirit. Paul finds this so puzzling that he decides to check and make sure these people are actually saved! "And [Paul] said to them, 'Into what then were you baptized?'" (verse 3).

When they say, "Into John's baptism," Paul quickly explains what they are missing:

> "John indeed baptized with a baptism of repentance, saying to the people that they should believe on Him who would come after him, that is, on Christ Jesus."
>
> When they heard this, they were baptized in the name of the Lord Jesus. And when Paul had laid hands on them, the Holy Spirit came upon them, and they spoke with tongues and prophesied. (verses 4–6)

How many baptisms do the believers in Ephesus ultimately experience? In this case, because they had repented and been baptized under John the

Baptist, they received at least three and possibly four: (1) John's water baptism of repentance, (2) baptism into the body of Christ through belief in "Him who would come after him, that is, on Christ Jesus," (3) water baptism by Paul "in the name of the Lord Jesus," and (4) baptism in the Holy Spirit through the laying on of Paul's hands.

Notice what happens when the Ephesian believers receive the baptism in the Holy Spirit: "The Holy Spirit came upon them, and they spoke with tongues and prophesied." We see this pattern repeated again and again throughout the book of Acts.

## THREE WITNESSES IN HEAVEN AND ON EARTH

In fact, we can find these three baptisms throughout the Bible. For example, look at 1 John 5:7: "There are three that bear witness in heaven: the Father, the Word, and the Holy Spirit; and these three are one." Of course, "the Word" is a reference to Jesus.

Do you believe what 1 John 5:7 says—that the Father, Jesus, and the Holy Spirit "are one"? In other words, do you believe in the Trinity? I suspect you do. This verse says that these three all "bear witness in heaven." Of course, we aren't in heaven right now. We're on earth. So who or what is bearing witness here on earth? The next verse tells us,

> And there are three that bear witness on earth: the Spirit, the water,
> and the blood; and these three agree as one. (verse 8)

Here we have the three baptisms in reverse order! The three "witnesses" on earth are the Holy Spirit baptism, water baptism, and salvation through the blood of Jesus Christ. Each one of these baptisms represents a distinct work of grace God wants to do in our hearts and lives.

*Salvation* is a miraculous work of grace upon the heart. This truth is obvious and noncontroversial. The entire evangelical world agrees with what Ephesians 2:8–9 clearly states: "By grace you have been saved through faith, and that not of yourselves; it is the gift of God, not of works, lest anyone should boast." No one argues against what 2 Corinthians 5:17 promises: "If anyone is in Christ, he is a new creation; old things have passed away; behold, all things have become new."

*Water baptism* is a work of grace, in and upon the heart of man. Of course, being baptized in water doesn't save us. You can be saved, die, and go straight to heaven without ever being baptized in water. Rather, the act of being immersed in water is symbolic in an outward way of what has happened to us inwardly, symbolizing the death and burial of our old sinful self and the raising up of the "new creation" mentioned in 2 Corinthians 5:17. Yet water baptism is more than *just* a symbol. The Bible teaches that water baptism is a New Covenant counterpart to circumcision in the Old Covenant. Circumcision was a literal cutting away of the flesh. In a similar way, when we obediently submit ourselves to water baptism, a work of grace happens, causing a cutting away of the carnal (flesh) in our hearts. A real change takes place.

The same is true with a believer's baptism in the Holy Spirit. This act releases within us the supernatural empowerment to do all that God calls us to do. As we've seen, Jesus commanded His disciples to wait in Jerusalem until the promised Holy Spirit came. Why? Because, in Jesus's own words, they would be clothed in heavenly power (see Luke 24:49); receive empowerment to be witnesses for Him all over the world (see Acts 1:8); and do even greater things than He had done (see John 14:12).

> This act **RELEASES** within us the **SUPERNATURAL** empowerment to do all that God **CALLS** us to **DO**.

Let me condense and summarize these three "witnesses" in a personal way. When I was saved, I became a new person. When I was baptized in water, the old person was cut off. And when I was baptized in the Holy Spirit, I received the power to walk in the new. That third baptism makes a huge difference! For years, I tried to live in victory and power and purity. However, I experienced little but failure and frustration. After I received that third baptism, everything changed.

For example, the wonderful intimacy with the Holy Spirit that I began to enjoy became so precious to me that I would shrink back at the thought of doing anything that would grieve Him.

Because God's Word was now alive to me in new ways, I suddenly found scriptures coming to my mind at critical times of need or temptation. And that sense of "anointing" I had frequently experienced when in the pulpit quickly came to be a part of my daily life—at the grocery store, on the golf course, and most important, inside the walls of my own home.

Ask my wife, Debbie, if receiving the baptism in the Holy Spirit made a difference in her husband's life.

## WHAT ABOUT YOU?

I want you to ask yourself an important question: "Have I experienced only two baptisms?" In other words, have you only been baptized into the body of Christ when you were saved, and then baptized in water?

Have you ever experienced an immersion in the Holy Spirit that brought supernatural power and help into your life? By now we can agree that this third baptism doesn't happen at the moment of salvation. Yes, the Holy Spirit baptized you into Jesus when you were saved. But now Jesus has something reciprocal He wants to do. He wants to baptize you with power from on high. Why in the world would anyone say, "Thanks, but no thanks," to that?

Many Christians are living lives of defeat, frustration, and failure, as I did before I opened my heart and mind to this third baptism. I've tried living without the Holy Spirit's power, but I wouldn't go back to that way of living for all the money in the world. It's too wonderful to have God the Holy Spirit as a best friend.

> The Holy Spirit **EMPOWERED** Moody so **GREATLY** that when he would just **WALK** through factories, the **WORKERS** would fall on their **FACES** and be **SAVED**.

Remember the story of the evangelist D. L. Moody I told earlier? Moody later said that he was never the same after the day he was baptized in the Holy Spirit. He realized that almost everything he had accomplished in ministry prior to that moment had been done in the power of his own limited flesh. Afterward, he saw tens of thousands saved in revivals everywhere he went. Some biographers say the Holy Spirit empowered Moody so greatly that when he would just walk through factories, the workers would fall on their faces and be saved.

"And you shall receive power when the Holy Spirit has come upon you." (Acts 1:8). That's the biblical truth that transformed the life and ministry of D. L. Moody. It could only happen after he humbled himself enough to acknowledge that he needed another baptism.

What about you?

# Empowered to Live

I'm constantly amazed at how technology advances and changes so rapidly. I remember when people used to write to the American Automobile Association (AAA) office in some far-flung city months before leaving on a summer vacation. They gave their home address, listed attractions they wanted to see, and noted the cities where they planned to stay overnight. Several weeks later, the whole family would excitedly open the package from AAA filled with hand-marked maps of suggested routes and highlighted guides of AAA-rated motels.

Of course, many people now rely on a GPS system built right into their cars to get them where they want to go. I often use MapQuest.com. Same principle—enter a starting point and destination, and seconds later MapQuest provides both a map and turn-by-turn directions, listing miles between each turn, along with street names and landmarks to watch for. Of course, if you happen to be visiting a strange city and don't really know where you're starting from, your directions are totally useless.

Every process needs a starting point. The Christian life begins with the transformational moment of being born again. In a similar way, the Spirit-filled life begins with the transformational moment of being baptized in the Holy Spirit.

We've already examined numerous New Testament examples of this principle of three baptisms. However, if this is a valid biblical truth (and it is), we should also look for some examples of Old Testament foreshadowing and symbolism of the same principle. Let me point out a few to consider.

## ABRAHAM DOES HIS JOB: HE BELIEVES!

We can start with Abraham. Genesis 12:1 begins his story by telling us,

> Now the LORD had said to Abram:
>    "Get out of your country,
>    From your family
>    And from your father's house,
>    To a land that I will show you."

This call for Abraham to leave his native country is a salvation-like experience. When we are saved, we leave the kingdom where we were born and become citizens of a new kingdom. This is exactly how Paul describes being born again: "For He rescued us from the domain of darkness, and transferred us to the kingdom of His beloved Son" (Colossians 1:13, NASB).

God speaks to Abraham, called Abram at this point in his life, and calls him into relationship. Abram responds to this call and leaves his old life behind. Paul confirms this in Romans 4:3 by stating that when God called him, "Abraham believed God, and it was accounted to him for righteousness."

We find the next big milestone in Abraham's life in Genesis 15:17–18:

> And it came to pass, when the sun went down and it was dark, that behold, there appeared a smoking oven and a burning torch that passed between those pieces. On the same day the LORD made a covenant with Abram, saying:
>    "To your descendants I have given this land."

This describes a "covenant cutting" ceremony between God and Abram. I believe this event is a type of water baptism, which represents a cutting away of our fleshly desires. Allow me to explain further.

In ancient times two parties entered into sacred covenant by sacrificing an animal, cutting it in half, and then placing the two halves on the ground with space between the halves. The two parties walked between the halves as a part of swearing an unbreakable life-and-death oath of faithfulness. The act symbolized that the two parties were in covenant by blood.

Abram understood the significance of what God was doing when He instructed him to prepare this covenant sacrifice. Abram fully expected to walk between those halves with God. Yet God did something wonderful. He put Abram to sleep. Then a smoking oven and a burning torch appeared. I believe the oven is symbolic of the Father because the "true bread" comes from Him (see John 6:32), and the torch represents the Son because He is the light of the world. In other words, the Son stepped in to represent Abram in the covenant agreement. Why? Because God knew Abram, as a fallen and sinful man, couldn't possibly keep his side of the contract. Abram's only role was to "believe"—to have faith in the Son's participation and covenant-keeping on his behalf.

Please get this next point. God the Father and God the Son made a covenant through the cross two thousand years ago. The Son stepped in to fulfill our part of the agreement, because as sinful and fallen people, we couldn't do it on our own. To receive the benefits and blessings of this covenant, our only role is to believe.

> To **RECEIVE** the benefits and blessings of this **COVENANT**, our only role is to **BELIEVE**.

You might be thinking, *That's great, Robert, but how is what Abram experienced a type of water baptism?* It symbolizes baptism because the parties had to "pass through" the pieces that represented death. The sacrificed animal signified that if either party violated the covenant, they would die. In the same way, passing through the waters of baptism signifies a type of death to the old self.

## PROMISES FOR THE CHILDREN OF ISRAEL

Another Old Testament event illuminates this idea more deeply. You'll recall that the children of Israel departed Egypt after the blood of a lamb on the doorposts of their homes caused the angel of death to pass over their houses. The resulting death of the firstborn throughout Egypt served as the last straw for Pharaoh, and he finally agreed to let the Israelites leave. Just like Abraham, they "went out" of the pagan country they'd called home for more than four hundred years and headed toward a land of promise and blessing. In other words, the leaving of Egypt symbolizes salvation.

What happened immediately after that? The Israelites found themselves backed up against the Red Sea with Pharaoh's chariots bearing down on them. Moses used his staff to part the sea, and the Israelites "passed through" the waters, which had suddenly been cut in half. They walked between the two halves of water to safety. When Pharaoh's army entered the sea, however, the halves came back together and drowned them all—cutting off the flesh of the old life the Israelites were leaving behind. We are told in 1 Corinthians 10 that the passing through the sea represents water baptism.

## THE HOLY SPIRIT EMPOWERS ABRAHAM

Let's jump back to Abraham's story to look at an event that symbolizes Holy Spirit baptism. Genesis 17:5 states, "No longer shall your name be called Abram, but your name shall be Abraham; for I have made you a father of many nations."

You might be wondering, *What does a simple name change have to do with Holy Spirit baptism?* The answer is beautifully simple. The change from Abram to Abraham required putting the "ha" sound in the middle. There are no vowels in written Hebrew, so in the original language, God added the equivalent of the Hebrew letter *h*. In Hebrew this letter is also the word *ruah*, which represents "spirit," "breath," and "wind." Think about how you have to breathe out and create wind to make the sound "ha."

Throughout Scripture the word *ruah* is used to signify the Spirit, life, and power of God. In Genesis 1:2 we learn that "the *Spirit of God* was hovering over the face of the waters" back at the very beginning of creation. In Exodus 31:3, when God tells Moses about a skilled craftsman He has anointed to work on fixtures for the tabernacle, God states, "I have filled him with the *Spirit of God,* in wisdom, in understanding, in knowledge, and in all manner of workmanship." This word appears over and over in the Old

Testament. With Abram, God literally opens up Abram's name and pours
*ruah*—His own Spirit—into it. And it becomes Abra-*ha*-m!

What's more, God wasn't just
changing Abram's name. God was
changing his identity to reflect the reality that He had changed the man. God
breathed on him and Abraham became
a forerunner of the Spirit-filled life.

> To **TURN** Sarai into
> Sarah, God had to first
> **TAKE** out the *i*. We can
> **LEARN** a lot of **TRUTH**
> in that little **DETAIL**.

Abraham had a wife named Sarai.
God put his Spirit-breath in Sarai's
name as well:

> Then God said to Abraham, "As for Sarai your wife, you shall not
> call her name Sarai, but Sarah shall be her name." (Genesis 17:15)

You'll also note that to turn Sarai into Sarah, God had to first take out
the *i*. We can learn a lot of truth in that little detail. Receiving the baptism
in the Holy Spirit requires humility and selflessness. Prideful and self-
centered people simply don't yield themselves to the baptism in the Holy
Spirit. We have to remove the willful "I" from our hearts before God can
pour in His empowering "ha."

## THE HOLY SPIRIT EMPOWERS THE ISRAELITES

What about Moses and the Israelites leaving Egypt? Did they experience a
baptism in the Holy Spirit in their journey to the land of promise?

In Joshua 3 we find the account of the Israelites crossing the Jordan
River into Canaan, the Promised Land. The Lord miraculously parted the
water, as with the Red Sea, and the people crossed over on dry land. After
they crossed over, there were battles to fight and land to take. But the Israelites were supernaturally empowered to win and succeed. In fact, as long as
they didn't grieve the Lord through disobedience or rebellion, they received
supernatural empowerment for every task.

## Amazing Examples, Sound Advice

In case you think I'm stretching things a bit by saying these Old Testament events are symbolic of baptism, allow me to call a witness to the stand to testify—the apostle Paul:

> Moreover, brethren, I do not want you to be unaware that all our fathers were under the cloud, all passed through the sea, all were baptized into Moses in the cloud and in the sea. (1 Corinthians 10:1–2)

Paul points out that the children of Israel symbolically experienced all three baptisms. They were "baptized into Moses in the cloud and in the sea."

- *Baptized into Moses.* For the Israelites, Moses was the deliverer, just as Jesus became the ultimate Deliverer of all humanity. In fact, Acts 3:22–26 compares Moses and Jesus—pointing out that Jesus fulfilled the prophecy in Deuteronomy 18 that predicts the rise of another Deliverer like Moses from among the Jewish people.
- *In the sea.* As we discussed earlier, this refers to the crossing of the Red Sea by the Israelites and represents water baptism.
- *In the cloud.* What did the cloud represent? The Holy Spirit. The children of Israel were led by a cloud by day and a pillar of fire by night, just as the Holy Spirit leads us today. Of course the Israelites could choose whether or not to follow the cloud's leading. In the same way, we must choose to follow the leading of the Holy Spirit if we want to benefit from His wise and all-knowing leadership and empowerment.

A few verses later, Paul gives some sound advice about what to do with all this information: "Now these things became our examples" (1 Corinthians 10:6), and, "Now all these things happened to them as examples, and they were written for our admonition" (verse 11).

*Admonition* means "instruction." Paul is explaining that the three-baptism experiences of Abraham, Moses, and the children of Israel should serve as examples to us and are provided for our instruction.

## ONE MORE EXAMPLE

If it's true that God provides these examples for our instruction, what example are you following? The Word of God clearly teaches that we should be baptized into the Deliverer, the water, and the cloud. But in case you're still struggling a bit, allow me to show you one additional picture in the Old Testament.

Are you familiar with the tabernacle of Moses? The tabernacle is the portable tent complex that God instructed Moses and the Israelites to construct as they wandered in the wilderness. He provided incredibly detailed instructions about how they were to build, lay out, and furnish the structure. The tabernacle had an outer court, an interior space called the holy place, and then a smaller space within that called the Most Holy or the Holy of Holies. The ark of the covenant was kept in the Holy of Holies, the place of God's manifested presence. No one could simply enter the Most Holy off the street. Coming into the presence of God as a sinful and fallen person would be fatal. The sheer glory and purity of God would kill anyone who tried.

According to the strict instructions God gave Moses, Aaron, and the Levitical priests, a high priest needed to go through three stations or tasks before he could enter the Holy of Holies. Imagine that—*three* things!

First, the priest had to sacrifice a spotless, unblemished lamb on the altar. Next, the priest went to a basin filled with water, called a laver, where he washed and made himself ceremonially clean. Finally, the priest went to a place where he was anointed with oil. Only then could the priest approach the presence of God in the Holy of Holies.

> **GOD** essentially **SAYS**, "If you want to **ENJOY** the **FULLNESS** of My presence and **POWER**, **YOU** need to **COME** the way I've prescribed."

I'm sure I don't have to explain the symbolic significance of these steps to you. The blood of the spotless lamb is clearly a reference to salvation through the blood of Jesus. The washing with water at the laver represents water baptism. And oil has always been a symbol for the Holy Spirit in Scripture. The pouring of anointing oil over the head of the priest is an amazing picture of the anointing upon a believer being baptized in the Holy Spirit.

In spite of the clear instructions regarding the three baptisms we've been discussing, here's what I see many believers do. They want to experience the blessings and benefits of God's presence. So in essence, they enter the tabernacle and say, "Yes, I receive the blood of the Lamb. And yes, I'll wash with water. But I don't think I want to have anything to do with that anointing oil. I've seen some weird things with that. I'd like to skip that step. Yet I still want to go on into the presence of God."

That's not smart. As we've seen throughout our discussion, God essentially says, "If you want to enjoy the fullness of My presence and power, you need to come the way I've prescribed."

The blood of the lamb, the laver, and the anointing oil clearly represent the three baptisms: salvation, when the Holy Spirit baptizes us into the body of Christ; water baptism, when we are baptized in water after we receive Jesus as our Lord and Savior; and Spirit baptism, when Jesus baptizes us with power from on high, the Holy Spirit!

## SUMMING UP

Have you experienced three baptisms? Is it possible that you are a born-again believer who has missed on one or two baptisms? Many people were sprinkled or christened as infants, gave their lives to Jesus later on in life, but were never water baptized by immersion afterward. If that's true for you, you're missing out on the blessings that come from being obedient in that area. A wonderful work of grace is available to you through water baptism.

Or perhaps you have neglected or even resisted the third baptism of the anointing oil of the Holy Spirit. If so, I urge you to set aside whatever obstacles of pride or stubbornness have kept you from yielding yourself wholly and fully to all God has for you. Taking this step is as simple as asking and receiving. You can do that now, right where you are. Ask Jesus, our wonderful Lord and Savior, to baptize you in the Holy Spirit right now.

# PART 5

# The Giver

# Acts of Grace

A friend of mine was thinking about naming his soon-to-be-born daughter Charis (pronounced with a hard *k* sound, as in *kare-iss*). He and his wife thought it was a pretty name, and they liked the meaning of "grace" that's behind it.

When my friend told me they were considering this name, I responded by saying, "Let me encourage you *not* to do that."

Obviously puzzled why I'd have an opinion about his future daughter's name, he gave me a funny look and asked, "Why not?"

"Because your last name is Maddox," I replied. "Do your really want your daughter's name to be Charis Maddox?" Because he still looked confused, I said the name out loud and faster one more time. The light bulb went on for him when he heard how much "Charis Maddox" sounded like "Charismatics."

Mercifully, they chose a different name for their baby girl, because as I'll explain shortly, the word *charismatic* has negative vibes with some people.

## GIFTS OF GRACE

Inside the word *charismatic* is *charisma*—a word we borrowed whole from the Greeks (the plural in Greek is *charismata*). When the Greeks used *charisma* in a sentence, they weren't referring to charm or personality. For them, *charisma* literally meant "grace gift." In other words, it described a gift someone gave you because you had found undeserved favor in his eyes.

Of course, when you think about it, all true gifts come by grace. If you earn what you receive in any way, it isn't really a gift. Instead, it would be a payment or compensation. By definition, a gift is an act of grace.

That makes the word *charismata* (grace gifts) a little redundant. However, God put it in the Bible this way to emphasize something important. It's as if *charismata* is a double declaration of the truth that we don't deserve or earn the things God places in our lives. He gives us His grace gifts simply because He loves us and He is good.

All through this book we've seen that the transformative power of the Holy Spirit in our lives is enormous. Yet His power only operates to the degree that we allow Him to change us. Having the Holy Spirit's power available to us isn't the same as making ourselves available to the Holy Spirit's life-changing power. We have to yield. Our stubborn, prideful selves have to submit. We have to *receive.*

As we continue our look at the Holy Spirit, we'll next explore the truth that Jesus sent us a helper and friend who comes bearing gifts of grace.

### CHARISMATIC CONFUSION

As with the label *Pentecostal,* the word *charismatic* carries a range of meanings. In the wider culture we use the word *charisma* to describe people with a lot of personality and appeal. Many successful politicians are described as "charismatic." A Hollywood star might have a great deal of "charisma."

When we use the term in Christian circles, *charismatic* carries a completely different set of connotations. We talk about Charismatics (using a capital *C*) as well as the Charismatic movement.

In the eyes of some people, Charismatics participate in a worship style that utilizes contemporary music while raising their hands once in a while. For others, Charismatics are those who believe God still miraculously heals people today just as He did when the Bible was being written—and that it's appropriate for His people to ask Him to do so. Others consider anyone who acknowledges an active role for the Holy Spirit in the lives of believers today to be Charismatic.

This range of definitions creates lots of opportunities for confusion and misunderstanding. For example, in the first few years after founding the church I pastor, people frequently asked me, "So, what kind of church is it? Is it Charismatic?" I always prefaced my answer with, "Well, that depends on what you mean by Charismatic."

I'd continue, "If you want to know if we believe in the present person and work of the Holy Spirit, then the answer is a definite yes. If you want to know if we believe that all the gifts of the Holy Spirit mentioned in the New Testament are still available and operating today, again the answer is yes. But some things that you might have seen on television or in other churches that have become associated with the word *charismatic,* I'm not comfortable with. That's definitely *not* who we are as a church."

## How the Bible Defines Charisma

As I mentioned, the word *charisma* or *charismata* appears numerous times in the New Testament in reference to the Holy Spirit's work in the life of a believer. The word is used any time you read about "gifts of the Spirit." Just so we start our exploration on the same page, allow me to offer what I consider a biblical definition of *charisma:*

Charisma is the instantaneous enablement of the Holy Spirit in the life of any believer to exercise a gift for the edification of others.*

> Many **PEOPLE** are confused and **IGNORANT** about spiritual **GIFTS.**

This is probably the best definition I know for *charisma.* Notice it says "any believer." This supernatural enablement, which many call spiritual gifts, isn't reserved for people in full-time ministry or for some kind of ultra-superspiritual Christians.

Even in the body of Christ, many people are confused and ignorant about spiritual gifts. I'm not intending to be unkind by using the word

---

* Bill Konstantopolous, "The Manifestations of the Holy Spirit," Sermon Index, June 19, 2006, www.sermonindex.net/modules/newbb/viewtopic.php?topic_id=11094&forum=34&0.

*ignorant.* I mean that many people operate without truly and accurately understanding what the Bible teaches about this vitally important subject.

This problem isn't new. Paul begins 1 Corinthians 12 with the words, "Now concerning spiritual gifts, brethren, I do not want you to be ignorant" (verse 1). Apparently, a lot of confusion and ignorance about spiritual gifts also existed two thousand years ago.

Paul actually uses the phrase "now concerning" six different times in 1 Corinthians. In spite of the name this book has in our Bibles, 1 Corinthians actually wasn't Paul's first letter to the church at Corinth. In 1 Corinthians 5:9, Paul mentions a letter he'd written previously that apparently sparked a number of controversies in the church and generated a lot of questions in the minds of the Corinthian believers. They wrote back to Paul to ask for clarification on these issues.

He begins 1 Corinthians 7 by saying, "Now concerning the things of which you wrote to me" (verse 1).

In 1 Corinthians 7:25, Paul writes, "Now concerning virgins."

Paul begins 1 Corinthians 8 with, "Now concerning things offered to idols" (verse 1).

This continues throughout the whole letter. (Perhaps this is why the Holy Spirit saw fit not to have Paul's earlier letter included in the canon of Scripture. Obviously, it provoked more questions than it answered and shed more heat than light on the problems these believers were facing.)

> The two **IDOLS** Corinthian citizens **WORSHIPED** most were **MONEY** and **SEX**.

In addition to facing confusion, the church in Corinth wasn't a Jewish congregation. These were Gentile converts. Also, the city of Corinth was a wealthy but wicked port city at the intersection of several key sea-trade routes. Numerous temples to various Greek and Roman gods dotted the city, including the massive temple of the goddess Aphrodite, which is said to have employed more than one thousand ritual prostitutes. The two idols Corinthian citizens worshiped most were money and sex.

With this background in mind, let's jump back to what Paul writes to these believers about spiritual gifts: "Now concerning spiritual gifts, brethren, I do not want you to be ignorant" (1 Corinthians 12:1).

Obviously, the believers within the church had experienced some confusion about how spiritual gifts work and how they should be utilized within the church—particularly during public worship services. With the above phrase Paul begins a section of instruction and explanation that runs three chapters in the Bible. Let's look at the first of these verses and then break them down for additional insight:

> There are diversities of gifts, but the same Spirit. There are differences of ministries, but the same Lord. And there are diversities of activities, but it is the same God who works all in all. (verses 4–6)

Note the phrases "the same Spirit," "the same Lord," and "the same God." This is a reference, I believe, to the Holy Spirit, the Son, and the Father, respectively. Paul's message is, "There are many different gifts (*charismata*), and many different 'ministries' and 'activities' within which those gifts can be expressed—but the same triune God is still behind all of them."

> He **GIVES** us **GIFTS** so we can be a **BLESSING** to **OTHERS**.

The Greek word translated "activities" in the verse above is *energema*, which means "the thing that is produced" or "the outcome." *Energema* is also the Greek root of our English word *energy*. Paul is teaching that when you plug a spiritual "gift" into a "ministry," you get a powerful "result."

What kind of outcomes will this process produce? Paul tells us in the very next verse: "But the manifestation of the Spirit is given to each one for the profit of all" (verse 7).

Why does the Holy Spirit give spiritual gifts to us? So those gifts can be released in "ministries," "for the profit of all." He gives us gifts so we can be a blessing to others. Notice also that these gifts are given to "each one." Not some. Not most. "Each one" of us is the recipient of these spiritual gifts in various times and places if we are born again and are willing to be used by God to bring about "the profit of all."

## THE OWNER OF THE GIFTS

All of this prompts these two important questions: What kinds of gifts? What do these gifts look like? In the next few verses, Paul lists nine of them:

> For to one is given the word of wisdom through the Spirit, to another the word of knowledge through the same Spirit, to another faith by the same Spirit, to another gifts of healings by the same Spirit, to another the working of miracles, to another prophecy, to another discerning of spirits, to another different kinds of tongues, to another the interpretation of tongues. But one and the same Spirit works all these things, distributing to each one individually as He wills. (1 Corinthians 12:8–11)

We can categorize these nine gifts into three distinct groups, and we'll examine this in greater detail shortly. However, allow me to explain something about the gifts that isn't widely understood. Some people read this list and assume that God looks at one person and says, "Hmm, I think I'll give Mark the gift of the word of knowledge." Then He looks at Susan and says, "I think I'll give her the gift of faith." The assumption is that the Holy Spirit assigns one gift to these people for the rest of their lives and they then own that gift forever.

> The Holy Spirit **OWNS** all the **GIFTS**, all the **TIME**.

That's actually not how the giving of these gifts works. The Holy Spirit owns all the gifts, all the time. When I was baptized in the Holy Spirit, I didn't just receive one gift, once and for always. Through the years He has bestowed all these gifts into my life for special moments in certain circumstances. I don't get to choose which gift I want at which time. As the verse above reminds us, He distributes "to each one individually as He wills."

Later in his letter to the Corinthians, Paul summarizes what will occur when the believers assemble:

> How is it then, brethren? Whenever you come together, each of you has a psalm, has a teaching, has a tongue, has a revelation, has an interpretation. Let all things be done for edification. (1 Corinthians 14:26)

The obvious message here is that *each* person may come with *all* that Paul mentions—a psalm, teaching, tongue, revelation, and interpretation—because of the phrase "each of you."

That's why I believe any Christian at any time might receive a word of knowledge. Any believer at any time might receive a gift of faith or a miracle or a healing. The Holy Spirit decides, because the gifts belong to Him and He distributes them all through us individually for the benefit of all.

Over the next few chapters, we'll take a brief look at the three broad categories of gifts. Then we'll explore the operation of these gifts in greater detail. For now, we only need to have a general familiarity with them, especially before we delve into the topic that might be the most controversial and problematic for some people. Of course, I'm referring to the issue of speaking in tongues.

For now, let's briefly acquaint ourselves with the discerning gifts, the declarative gifts, and the dynamic gifts.

# 14

# The Discerning Gifts

I was once in a cafeteria eating a meal with my wife, Debbie, when I observed a muscular fellow and a woman I later learned was his wife carrying their trays to an empty table near us.

The moment my eyes fell on this gentleman, I knew something about him. I recognized this knowledge as coming from the Holy Spirit because I'd never seen this man before in my life. I also knew that the Holy Spirit doesn't give us such knowledge without good reason. God loved this man and wanted to help him.

Over the years I've learned how to act on supernatural insights like these without seeming weird or creepy. As I've said, my friend the Holy Spirit isn't weird. He just wants to see people free and whole. I got up and walked over to this couple's table and said, "Excuse me, you don't know me. But may I ask you a question?"

The man looked a little startled, but he said, "Sure."

"Have you ever lifted weights?" I asked. Now this wasn't a supernatural insight on my part. I just needed a humorous icebreaker. Anyone looking at this beefy man would have deduced that he spent a lot of time in the gym. But I later learned that he was actually a former bodybuilder who had won a Mr. America title at one point.

He and his wife chuckled, and then he said, "Uh, yeah, I've done a little weightlifting."

"Well, this might sound strange to you," I followed up. "But I believe God told me something very personal and important about you. I wonder if you'd mind if I shared it with you."

His eyes got very big, and he looked at his wife for a moment. Then he said, "Sure, pull up a chair."

"The Holy Spirit showed me a picture of you when you were a young boy. I saw you sitting in your grandmother's lap, and you were crying. She told you that God could make you strong like Samson if you promised to serve Him. I saw you make that commitment to serve God and honor Him with your life. Well, God told me to tell you that He kept His end of the deal, but you didn't keep your promise."

> "I **PROMISED** God that if He'd make me **STRONG**, I'd **SERVE** Him all my **LIFE**."

The man looked at me for a couple of seconds with such a blank look on his face that I wondered if I'd missed it. This certainly wasn't a guy I wanted to offend! But just as I was beginning to pray for a quick escape, his chin began to quiver and big tears started rolling down his face. He looked at his wife, and she began to cry as well. As it turned out, he'd just been telling her that story!

He said, "Sir, I was raised by my grandmother. My father left when I was born, and my mother left a few years later. One day when I was about eight, some boys were throwing rocks at me, just to be mean. One hit me in the head and put a gash in it, and I went home crying. That's when my grandmother sat me in her lap and told me the story of Samson. I promised God that if He'd make me strong, I'd serve Him all my life. I was just telling my wife that I've been thinking about that promise lately, but I didn't really even know how to approach God."

I led them both to the Lord on the spot, and they were baptized the next week. In this instance, the Holy Spirit gave me a gift of a word of knowledge. As we've seen, this gift is listed in 1 Corinthians 12:8–11 as one of nine spiritual gifts that the Spirit distributes to each believer as He "wills." This is yet another reminder that the Holy Spirit is a person—possessing a mind, will, and emotions. He chooses.

At the front end of that list, we find, "For to one is given the word of wisdom through the Spirit, to another the word of knowledge through the same Spirit" (1 Corinthians 12:8). The "word of wisdom" and the "word of knowledge." We can classify these two gifts of the Spirit under the discerning gifts. Another appropriate label would be the perceiving gifts. Either name fits because when these gifts operate, you are empowered to discern or perceive certain truths that can help another person. Keep in mind, these gifts are always given in order to bless and benefit others. And others will operate in these gifts to bless and benefit you!

## A Word of Knowledge

What do these gifts look like in operation? Let's begin with the gift the Spirit used to touch the life of that bodybuilder that day in the cafeteria—the "word of knowledge."

A word of knowledge is the Holy Spirit allowing you to know something specific that you didn't learn by natural means. It's a supernatural transfer of information you couldn't possibly know through natural processes.

Jesus operated in this gift all the time. Do you recall His encounter with the Samaritan woman at the well? She told Jesus that she wasn't married, and He responded by saying, "You have well said, 'I have no husband,' for you have had five husbands, and the one whom you now have is not your husband; in that you spoke truly" (John 4:17–18).

That was a pretty specific piece of information Jesus knew about a perfect stranger. Of course, you might be thinking that Jesus was God in human flesh and knew information like this because He was God. That's a com-

> Jesus, indeed, was **FULLY GOD** and fully man, but He didn't **LIVE** His life **ACCESSING** His **GODHOOD.**

mon assumption, but false. Jesus, indeed, was fully God and fully man, but He didn't live His life accessing His Godhood. Philippians 2 tells us He "emptied Himself" of all his rights and privileges as God, "taking the form of a bond-servant, and being made in the likeness of men" (verse 7, NASB).

Jesus didn't perform a single miracle until after the Holy Spirit descended upon Him immediately following His baptism. Repeatedly, Jesus told His disciples that He only said what He heard the Father saying and did what the Father, through the Holy Spirit, prompted Him to do (see Luke 4:1; John 5:19; 8:28). Jesus demonstrated what's possible for a person fully yielded and obedient to the Holy Spirit.

> Jesus demonstrated
> **WHAT'S POSSIBLE**
> for a **PERSON**
> fully **YIELDED** and
> **OBEDIENT** to
> the Holy Spirit.

By the way, the Holy Spirit didn't reveal the Samaritan woman's secret to Jesus to embarrass her. He spoke it to open her eyes because God loved her and wanted her to be free and whole. Gifts of the Spirit are always given to edify, to encourage, and to set captive people free.

This has certainly been my experience through the years with this wonderful gift, including my encounter with the former Mr. America. The power of a word of knowledge is one of the most exciting and rewarding incidents we can be a part of. And this gift is available to every believer who yields to the Holy Spirit and obeys His promptings.

## DISCERNING OF SPIRITS

Another gift on the list of nine found in 1 Corinthians 12:8–11, which falls under the category of discerning gifts, is what the Bible calls "discerning of spirits." This gift involves the Holy Spirit making a believer aware of the presence of a demonic spirit.

I hope you're not shocked to hear that demonic spirits are present in our world today. If allowed, they will influence people's thoughts, behavior, and attitudes. I don't believe that a demon hides under every rock, or that every time your spouse is in a bad mood, the devil is directly involved. But the Bible clearly teaches that demons do influence people from time to time, even Christians. I didn't say "possess"; I said "influence."

Also note that this gift is called "discerning of spirits," not "the gift of discernment." I can't tell you how many times I've heard someone claim to operate in "the gift of discernment." No such gift is mentioned in the Bible. In my experience, what people really mean by that is they have a knack for criticism and judgmentalism.

Of course we need discernment. All believers are encouraged to discern between good and evil. But that's not a spiritual gift. According to Hebrews 5:14 we discern with our natural senses: "But solid food belongs to those who are of full age, that is, those who by reason of use have their senses exercised to discern both good and evil." In other words, we learn to discern good and evil through common sense and maturity.

Discerning of spirits, on the other hand, is a gift bestowed by and through the Holy Spirit. The apostle Paul operates in this gift in Acts 16 where Luke, the writer of Acts, describes some of Paul and Silas's activities in a city called Philippi:

> Now it happened, as we went to prayer, that a certain slave girl possessed with a spirit of divination met us, who brought her masters much profit by fortune-telling. This girl followed Paul and us, and cried out, saying, "These men are the servants of the Most High God, who proclaim to us the way of salvation." And this she did for many days.
>
> But Paul, greatly annoyed, turned and said to the spirit, "I command you in the name of Jesus Christ to come out of her." And he came out that very hour. (verses 16–18)

How did Paul know that this girl had an evil spirit of fortune-telling attached to her? What she said wasn't evil. She followed Paul around shouting something that was actually true. However, just because her words were true didn't mean the source was godly. This girl was becoming a distraction to Paul's work, and he feared that his ministry was in danger of becoming associated with her.

When you **REBUKE** a spirit in the **NAME** of **JESUS CHRIST**, it has to **FLEE**.

After putting up with her for several days, he finally got fed up and cast the demon out of her. But he only knew a demon was present to be cast out because the Holy Spirit revealed it to him through the gift of discerning of spirits.

Think about that. If a demonic spirit were coming against your business or home or family, wouldn't it be good for the Holy Spirit to make you aware of that? Once we are aware of the Enemy's attack, we can simply take authority over it by the authority of the blood of Jesus. When you rebuke a spirit in the name of Jesus Christ, just as Paul did in the account above, it has to flee.

## A WORD OF WISDOM

The gifts of the Spirit are wonderful things. God gives good gifts to His children! Another one of the discerning gifts is "the word of wisdom." This gift of the Holy Spirit is simply a divine answer or solution for a particular question or challenge.

Sometimes the word of wisdom comes in knowing exactly the right thing to *say*. Jesus operated in this gift all the time. When confronted by a group of skeptics, who were sure they were going to trip up Jesus with a trick question, He would turn the tables on them every time.

At other times this gift results in knowing exactly the right thing to *do*. When Jesus and Peter are about to be late in paying the temple tax, Jesus gets a word of wisdom that solves the problem for both of them: "Go to the sea, cast in a hook, and take the fish that comes up first. And when you have opened its mouth, you will find a piece of money; take that and give it to them for Me and you" (Matthew 17:27). Peter obeys. Problem solved.

Paul was also a recipient of this gift on numerous occasions. In Acts 27 we find him as a prisoner of the Roman government on a ship headed for Rome. The ship ends up in a terrible storm and is about to sink. The hired crew of the ship is about to sneak off in the only lifeboat, which would leave Paul, his fellow prisoners, and their Roman guards behind. At the critical moment, as everyone else is panicking and paralyzed with fear, Paul knows just what to do. He tells the Roman guards the actions that will save them all. The guards listen to him, and all are saved as Paul had promised.

In John 9 we see a man whom Jesus had recently healed of blindness operating in this gift. This man had been blind from birth, and when he suddenly showed up with his sight, he underwent intense questioning by the religious leaders who were looking for an excuse to charge Jesus with a crime. This man was obviously a walking advertisement for the power and authority of Jesus, and the comfortable religious elites wanted the formerly blind man either quieted or discredited.

> This **MAN** was obviously a walking **ADVERTISEMENT** for the power and **AUTHORITY** of **JESUS**.

The Pharisees interview the healed man, but they don't like any of his answers, because he gives Jesus all the credit and glory. So they drag the parents in to be interviewed, who wisely play dumb. They say, "We know that this is our son, and that he was born blind; but by what means he now sees we do not know, or who opened his eyes we do not know. He is of age; ask him. He will speak for himself" (verses 20–21).

I like that. The man's parents say, "Why are you asking us? He's a grown man. Ask *him*!"

So, the religious leaders bring the healed man back in for another round of interrogation. These are highly educated and respected teachers of the Law. They are skilled debaters. They're confident they can trip up or outsmart an illiterate little nobody who'd been a beggar all his life. Yet the well-laid plans of the Pharisees fall apart as this "nobody" begins to operate in the word of wisdom in his answers:

> So they again called the man who was blind, and said to him, "Give God the glory! We know that this Man is a sinner."
>
> He answered and said, "Whether He is a sinner or not I do not know. One thing I know: that though I was blind, now I see."
>
> Then they said to him again, "What did He do to you? How did He open your eyes?"
>
> He answered them, "I told you already, and you did not listen. Why do you want to hear it again? Do you also want to become His disciples?"

Then they reviled him and said, "You are His disciple, but we are Moses' disciples. We know that God spoke to Moses; as for this fellow, we do not know where He is from."

The man answered and said to them, "Why, this is a marvelous thing, that you do not know where He is from; yet He has opened my eyes! Now we know that God does not hear sinners; but if anyone is a worshiper of God and does His will, He hears him. Since the world began it has been unheard of that anyone opened the eyes of one who was born blind. If this Man were not from God, He could do nothing." (John 9:24–33)

A former beggar, who had spent a brief time with Jesus, outwitted a whole panel of professional debaters. That's the Spirit's gift of the word of wisdom!

I've seen this amazing and helpful gift operate in and around me many times. God has used me to offer a word of wisdom to others on occasion. And I've benefitted from the gift as it has operated in others.

The word of wisdom, the word of knowledge, and the discerning of spirits— these are the discerning gifts. They are awesome, but the Holy Spirit has much, much more in His arsenal of blessing and empowerment.

# 15

# The Declarative Gifts

**M**aybe you saw the season of the television show *America's Got Talent* in which a ten-year-old phenomenon blew away the studio audience—and much of the rest of the world—with her voice. From the vocal cords of this tiny girl came a rich, warm, and rounded voice far beyond her years. In fact, with her larger-than-life voice performing opera arias, many people were shocked when she only placed second on the show! Obviously, little Jackie Evancho's voice was a unique physical gift.

While few of us have the gift of a unique singing voice, the Holy Spirit does give a set of spiritual gifts to believers that some theologians call the vocal gifts. I prefer to call them declarative gifts.

As we just explored, the discerning gifts involve a supernatural downloading of information to the mind. They allow you to know something you didn't learn by natural means. The declarative gifts each involve a form of declaration of divine truth or supernatural message.

Let's take a fresh look at that section of Paul's list. He says the Holy Spirit gives "to another prophecy...to another different kinds of tongues, to another the interpretation of tongues" (1 Corinthians 12:10). Here we have three unique and wonderful gifts—prophecy, various tongues, and interpretation of tongues. Let's take a brief look at each.

## PROPHETIC MESSAGES OF ENCOURAGEMENT

When some people hear the word *prophecy,* they immediately think in terms of predicting the future. A word of prophecy can certainly be something about a future event. But that's not always the case. When the Bible speaks of a word of prophecy, it simply means "a message of encouragement from God, delivered through a human vessel, to another person or persons."

Please notice three elements in that definition. First, a word of prophecy is a message of encouragement—not discouragement, not correction or rebuke, and not judgment. In 1 Corinthians 14:3, Paul provides the threefold role of prophecy: "But he who prophesies speaks edification and exhortation and comfort to men." A great way to test the validity of a prophetic word is to ask, "Did that word of prophecy bring edification, exhortation, or comfort to the hearer?"

The gift of prophecy is among the highest and most important of all the spiritual gifts the Holy Spirit bestows. In fact, just two verses earlier, Paul gives this command: "Pursue love, and desire spiritual *gifts*, but especially that you may prophesy" (verse 1).

Paul says that it's good to want the gifts the Holy Spirit gives. They're all wonderful, all exciting, and all beneficial to the body of Christ—but we are to especially desire to operate in the gift of prophecy. This obviously isn't a gift set aside for a holy few or for an elite class of supersaints. Scripture wouldn't exhort us all to desire the gift of prophecy if it wasn't available to all of us.

## MESSAGES IN UNKNOWN LANGUAGES

That brings us to the next of the declarative gifts, the wonderful gift of tongues. It's no accident that Satan seems to oppose this gift more than any of the other eight. The devil works overtime to sow doubt, confusion, and fear in the minds of believers concerning this gift of the Holy Spirit. But all we really need to know about the gift of tongues is that it's *a gift from God the Holy Spirit.* If the God who loves us and gave His beloved Son to die for us wants us to have this gift, why would we be afraid of it?

Many people fail to recognize the difference between the "gift of tongues," which the Holy Spirit bestows on certain occasions distributing it "as He wills," and the "prayer language" that believers receive when they are baptized in the Holy Spirit, whether they realize it and activate it or not. The *gift* of tongues is a message from God to others in a language unknown to the person through whom the message comes. I'll share more on this distinction between the gift of tongues and the grace of prayer language (praying in the Spirit) in the next chapter.

Much of what Paul writes in 1 Corinthians 14 is designed to give the church at Corinth instruction and guidelines about how gifts of the Spirit, especially the gift of tongues, should be utilized in their public worship services. You might recall that Paul wrote this

> If the **GOD** who **LOVES** us and **GAVE** His beloved Son to **DIE** for us **WANTS** us to have this gift, **WHY** would we be **AFRAID** of it?

letter because the church in Corinth had a lot of questions and confusion about how to handle certain issues. Paul begins this whole section back at the opening of chapter 12 with the words, "Now concerning spiritual gifts."

Apparently, this group of believers was very excited about the gift of tongues and practiced it a lot in their public worship services. But they were neglecting the expression of other spiritual gifts such as prophecy. As Paul points out, the problem is that unless someone interprets a message in tongues, other people in the congregation can't be encouraged, edified, or comforted. What's more, visitors in the service, especially unbelievers, might think you're a bunch of crazy people.

Paul addresses this by following 1 Corinthians 12, which is about spiritual gifts, with chapter 13, which is all about walking in love toward others. God loves people, and He wants His people to reflect and share that love for a lost and dying world. We can get so excited about the power of God flowing through our lives through the gifts of the Holy Spirit that we forget the reason those gifts were bestowed in the first place: love. Love must govern and drive everything we do—including the use of spiritual gifts. That's why Paul then follows his "love chapter" with 1 Corinthians 14, which begins like this:

> Pursue love, and desire spiritual gifts, but especially that you may
> prophesy. For he who speaks in a tongue does not speak to men but
> to God, for no one understands him; however, in the spirit he speaks

mysteries. But he who prophesies speaks edification and exhortation and comfort to men. He who speaks in a tongue edifies himself, but he who prophesies edifies the church. I wish you all spoke with tongues, but even more that you prophesied; for he who prophesies is greater than he who speaks with tongues, unless indeed he interprets, that the church may receive edification. (verses 1–5)

Through Paul, the Holy Spirit is telling the believers in Corinth (and us), "Make sure love motivates everything you do. By all means, hunger after spiritual gifts, but where public worship services are concerned, make prophecy the priority. Everyone will understand a prophetic word—even newcomers and unbelievers."

> **LOVE** must **GOVERN** and drive **EVERYTHING** we do—including the use of **SPIRITUAL** gifts.

Notice that Paul is careful not to dismiss tongues as a gift when he says, "I wish you all spoke with tongues." Rather, he is pointing out that the use of tongues should be carefully managed in public worship services. After emphasizing this point further in the next few verses, Paul gets to the bottom line: "Therefore let him who speaks in a tongue pray that he may interpret" (verse 13).

### INTERPRETING THE MESSAGES

This takes us to the third of the declarative gifts—interpretation of tongues. A biblical definition of this gift would be "understanding and expressing the thought or intent of a message in tongues." The keywords in that definition are "thought or intent."

When you receive the gift of interpretation of tongues, you get a supernatural understanding of the general gist of the message being communicated. This explains why the gift is called *interpretation* of tongues rather than *translation* of tongues.

Occasionally, people new to this phenomenon are puzzled by something. Sometimes, a fairly lengthy message in tongues will be followed by an interpretation that is significantly shorter, or vice versa. This makes much more sense when you think about the difference between translating a message in a foreign language and interpreting that message. A faithful translator will try to reproduce a message word for word in the native language of the hearer. All an interpreter has to do is convey the gist of the concepts.

Interpreters can choose to be long winded or extremely concise, depending upon the audience and the kinds of concepts they're trying to communicate. When my children were younger and all living at home, I got a vivid demonstration of this around the dinner table each night.

First, I would ask my son James how his day went. Ten hours of school and work and interaction with the wide world was usually condensed into one word: "Fine." Sometimes his answer was even more concise. If the day had

> Interpreters can **CHOOSE** to be long winded or extremely **CONCISE**, depending upon the **AUDIENCE** and the kinds of **CONCEPTS** they're trying to **COMMUNICATE**.

been challenging, he might just give me a facial expression that indicated "I've had better" and sort of grunt.

Then I would turn to his younger sister and pose the same question. Her response was usually something along the lines of, "Well, I woke up at 6:10, which means I overslept. I had set my alarm for 6:00. I must have hit the Snooze button without waking up enough to realize it, so I was running late before I even really got started, and then I made sure I took some tissues because I had a little bit of a sinus headache. I think it's because the weather has been sort of weird lately. So I took a shorter shower than normal because I was running late and didn't get my hair completely dry before I had to leave for first period, where we had a substitute today. That was lame because we didn't really do anything in class, but in second period we had a pop quiz, and I think I did pretty well, although my friend Ashley said she had brainlock and couldn't remember anything from the reading assignment..." And on would flow a torrent of detail like a mighty river—all in response to the same question about the same ten-hour span of time.

Both replies are interpretations of answers to the question, "How was your day?" Some things never change, of course. James is married now. He and his sweet bride were over for dinner not too long after they were married, and someone asked James how things were going at his job. When he responded with one of his classic facial replies, my daughter-in-law patted him on the hand and sweetly said, "Use syllables, honey."

The point is that the meaning of a long message in tongues can sometimes be perfectly encapsulated through a short interpretation. At the same time a short burst of tongues can deliver concepts and truths so deep and profound that it takes a long interpretation to do them justice.

We should also note that in 1 Corinthians 14, Paul declares that the gift of prophecy is superior to the gift of tongues in a public worship service. Let's look at the relevant portion of that passage again: "I wish you all spoke with tongues, but even more that you prophesied; for he who prophesies is greater than he who speaks with tongues, *unless...*" (verse 5). It's this "unless" I want you to notice. Unless, what? "...unless indeed he interprets, that the church may receive edification."

In a public worship service, where unbelievers and new Christians are present, prophecy is superior, because everybody can receive encouragement from the message. However, as Paul makes clear here, if the person who delivers a message in tongues goes on to also operate in the gift of interpretation of tongues, then everyone can be blessed by that message too. This puts an interpreted message on almost an equal footing with a prophetic message. Both are accessible by everyone in the service and will provide encouragement, exhortation, or comfort for everyone who hears them.

These are the declarative gifts, and they provide a tremendous blessing to the body of Christ. An encouraging word from God is a very good thing to receive!

# 16

# The Dynamic Gifts

Y ou might recall a news story from the early days of the U.S. invasion of Afghanistan about two young American missionary women held hostage by the Taliban.

Dayna Curry and Heather Mercer were believers who attended a Charismatic church in Waco, Texas, and volunteered to work in Afghanistan with a missionary group called Shelter Now. In August 2001—just weeks before the 9/11 attacks on America—the women were arrested by the Taliban for evangelizing. There were already serious concerns for their safety, but when the attacks on New York City and Washington were linked to Osama bin Laden, who was known to be a guest of the Taliban in Afghanistan, the anxiety among the women's loved ones increased. When the United States invaded Afghanistan in October of that year, there were grave fears that the Taliban would retaliate brutally against their young American hostages.

The women were eventually rescued by U.S. and anti-Taliban troops on November 15. Later, the women revealed that they had very different experiences while in captivity. Heather experienced all the fear, anxiety, and worry you might expect someone in this situation to feel. But Dayna found herself enveloped with an amazing level of calm and confidence for most of the harrowing experience. In an interview with *Christianity Today* magazine, she said, "I just had a supernatural peace most of the time. Actually, I'm going through way more stress now than I ever did in prison."*

---

* Stan Guthrie and Wendy Murray Zoba, "Double Jeopardy," *Christianity Today,* July 8, 2002, www.christianitytoday.com/ct/2002/july8/1.26.html.

What enabled Dayna to have such peace in the midst of the most terrifying of circumstances? She was a recipient of the gift of faith.

The gift of faith is one of the dynamic gifts. The name comes from Jesus's final words of instruction to His disciples before ascending to heaven. He told them to wait "in the city of Jerusalem until you are endued with power from on high" (Luke 24:49). You know by now that the source of the "power" Jesus promised was the outpoured Holy Spirit. Jesus stated this explicitly in His final hours on earth when He said, "But you shall receive power when the Holy Spirit has come upon you" (Acts 1:8).

The Greek word translated "power" in these verses is *dunamis* (sometimes spelled *dynamis*). It's the source of our English words *dynamite, dynamo,* and *dynamic.* So it's more than appropriate to call this next group of gifts from the Holy Spirit the dynamic gifts because they tend to display the power of God.

Going back to our list of the nine gifts of the Holy Spirit that Paul lists in 1 Corinthians 12, we find,

> But the manifestation of the Spirit is given to each one for the
> profit of all:...to another faith by the same Spirit, to another gifts
> of healings by the same Spirit, to another the working of miracles.
> (verses 7, 9–10)

Once again we have three distinct gifts in this grouping—faith, gifts of healings, and working of miracles. While these are three distinct gifts, they can produce similar results.

## SUPERNATURAL CONFIDENCE

Let's begin with the gift of faith. It might seem odd to think of faith as a gift of the Spirit, because everything about the Christian life involves faith. We're saved by grace through faith (see Ephesians 2:8–9), and Jesus repeatedly encourages us to have faith in God, implying that faith is a choice we make. So how can faith be a gift of the Holy Spirit that He distributes as He wills?

Paul is talking about an imparting of something distinct from the everyday faith we are called to exercise in our Christian walk. That's why some people refer to this as the "gift of special faith." I define the gift of faith as "a supernatural endowment of belief and confidence for a specific situation." Indeed, just as one woman missionary hostage in Afghanistan experienced great peace in terrifying circumstances because of the gift of faith, countless Christians can testify that in a moment of severe crisis or in a time of great need, they suddenly found themselves infused with a supernatural level of faith that everything would be okay. In turn, this level of faith opened the door to God's miraculous provision or deliverance. The faith they experienced in that moment was significantly higher and stronger than the faith they walk in day to day.

Jesus operated in all the spiritual gifts to a great degree, including the gift of special faith. Remember, He emptied Himself of His Godhood and lived as a Spirit-filled, Spirit-led man. We see Jesus displaying the gift of faith in Mark 4. You might recall the incident where Jesus and the disciples attempted to cross the Sea of Galilee in a fishing boat when a huge storm threatened to capsize the vessel. Jesus was fast asleep in the hold of the boat and seemed genuinely annoyed that His panicking disciples—most of them experienced fishermen and sailors—woke Him up.

> Jesus **OPERATED** in all the **SPIRITUAL** gifts to a **GREAT** degree.

In Acts 9 we see a man named Ananias who had the gift of faith. He receives instructions in a vision to go visit a man named Saul—the future apostle Paul—and lay hands on him to receive the baptism in the Holy Spirit. However, one little detail makes this assignment interesting, as we see in the opening words:

> Meanwhile, Saul was still breathing out murderous threats against the Lord's disciples. He went to the high priest and asked him for letters to the synagogues in Damascus, so that if he found any there who belonged to the Way, whether men or women, he might take them as prisoners to Jerusalem. (verses 1–2, NIV)

Saul is well known for ordering any Christians he encounters to be beaten or imprisoned. And Ananias suddenly gets instructions to pay Saul a visit and say, "Hi, I'm a Christian, and I'm here to lay hands on you!" But he boldly obeys. That takes the provision of the gift of faith.

What Ananias doesn't realize is that Saul has just been knocked off his feet and blinded by the glorified Jesus in a spectacular encounter on the road to Damascus. He is harmless and ready to receive.

## SUPERNATURAL HEALING

Just as Christians can receive the gift of faith today, the Holy Spirit also imparts what Paul calls "gifts of healings." These are "supernatural endowments of divine health."

Allow me to first elaborate on this gift by explaining what it is *not.* This is not the Holy Spirit depositing a special gifting in special people so they have the power to pray for people and see them healed. Whenever I hear someone proclaim they have the gift of healing, it troubles me. It suggests to me a shaky understanding of how the gifts and manifestations of the Holy Spirit operate. The Lord may indeed use a particular person consistently in the area of healing, but it is the Holy Spirit who owns the gift and distributes it individually, moment by moment, as He wills.

Of course, we rightly ask other believers to pray for us when we have some sort of sickness or infirmity in our bodies. Because the truth is that your neighbor in your small group Bible study is as likely to be used by the Holy Spirit to deliver God's healing power to you as the most famous television minister. However, this gift doesn't have to come through another person at all. Countless people have been healed miraculously in their prayer closets when all alone.

Anyone with even a casual familiarity with the Gospels knows that Jesus was always healing people. Everywhere He went, people were healed. We assume that Jesus performed these healings because He was God in human flesh—and He was. But we have no record of Jesus ever healing anyone prior to the Holy Spirit descending upon Him like a dove immediately after His baptism. Is it possible that Jesus was constantly healing the sick, opening blind eyes, and cleansing lepers because He was consistently endued with the gift of faith, the gift of healings, and the gift of miracles?

When Jesus gets back to His hometown sometime after He launches His public ministry, we're told, "Now He could do no mighty work there, except that He laid His hands on a few sick people and healed them. And He marveled because of their unbelief" (Mark 6:5–6). Clearly, there were times when the power to heal was more present in Jesus than at other times. You might recall the incident in Luke 5 when four men lowered their paralyzed friend down through a hole in the roof to get him to Jesus. Just prior to that, Luke says,

> Clearly, there were **TIMES** when the **POWER** to heal was **MORE PRESENT** in Jesus than at other times.

> Now it happened on a certain day, as He was teaching, that there were Pharisees and teachers of the law sitting by, who had come out of every town of Galilee, Judea, and Jerusalem. And the power of the Lord was present to heal them. (Luke 5:17)

Jesus received and operated in the gift of healings. His disciples did too, after they received the outpouring of the Holy Spirit on the Day of Pentecost. In fact, only a day or so after the Pentecost outpouring, Peter and John come across a beggar lying on the ground by the Gate Beautiful. He'd been born without the ability to walk, and some friends or family members had apparently carried him to this heavily trafficked spot every day so he could beg alms from others going up to the temple to worship or pray. Peter and John had probably passed by this man many times. But this day is different. When the man asks them for money, Peter says,

> "Silver and gold I do not have, but what I do have I give you: In the name of Jesus Christ of Nazareth, rise up and walk." And he took him by the right hand and lifted him up, and immediately his feet and ankle bones received strength. So he, leaping up, stood and

walked and entered the temple with them—walking, leaping, and praising God. (Acts 3:6–8)

This day was different because of the gift of healings imparted by the Holy Spirit poured out upon Peter and his fellow followers of Jesus.

Some people question whether the Holy Spirit still gives this gift. So I ask, has the Holy Spirit gone out of business, or is He on extended vacation? No! The gift of healings is still generously given today to those willing to receive it.

> Has the **HOLY SPIRIT** gone out of **BUSINESS**, or is He on extended **VACATION?**

I remember a time when our oldest child was just a newborn. He had jaundice and his skin had turned a sickly yellow. In my head I knew that healing was part of the atonement—meaning that Jesus bore our sicknesses as well as our sins on the cross (see Matthew 8:17). When you're a brand-new father and your baby is sick, healing takes on a new dimension of urgency. So I opened my Bible and began to read key scriptures clearly indicating that healing is part of our inheritance in Christ. As I did, I felt something rise up inside of me. I suddenly became overwhelmingly convinced that it was inappropriate and unlawful for sickness to be upon my baby boy.

I grabbed Debbie and we marched into his room where I laid my hands upon his little body and prayed for him to be healed. As Debbie will attest, when I finished, we watched Josh's skin color return to normal. This didn't happen because I'm called to full-time ministry. It occurred because the Holy Spirit gives gifts liberally to all.

## SUPERNATURALLY ALTERED CIRCUMSTANCES

In the same way, the gift called the working of miracles isn't deposited in just a special few people who carry it for the rest of their lives. The power to see a miracle take place is available to all believers, and the Holy Spirit distributes this gift as He wills in momentary situations.

I define the gift of the working of miracles as "divine intervention that alters circumstances." Is this something you'd like to experience? Would you be blessed if, from time to time, the miraculous power of God turned around a negative situation? If so, I want you to know that God is still working miracles. God is immutable—meaning He never changes. He's the same yesterday, today, and forever. He worked miracles in the days of the Old Testament as well as in the days of the New Testament, and He still works miracles today.

As long as God is on His throne, miracles will happen. And I can assure you, He's still on His throne.

## An Abundance of Giving

Please notice that these last two gifts of the Holy Spirit are listed in plural form. Scripture calls them the gift of *healings* and the gift of the working of *miracles*. This communicates that plenty of these gifts are available, and lets us know that every healing and every miracle is important to God. In other words, we can be certain of God's care for individuals.

As with other gifts of the Spirit, these dynamic gifts aren't just for a special few. God didn't hold a heavenly lottery to randomly select a handful of His people around the planet to experience miracles in their lives. If only a few people can see miracles happen and I need a miracle, I'm in trouble if I can't get to one of these special people. Thank God, the truth is that the gift of miracles is available to all people who have the Holy Spirit working inside. And an intimate, personal relationship with Him is available to every believer.

This explains why Jesus told His disciples it was better for them if He went away. In His earthly form, He could only be in one place at any one time. But the outpouring of the Holy Spirit upon human flesh on the Day of Pentecost was one of the most beneficial and important events in human history, making possible the extraordinary statement of Jesus in John 14:12:

> Most assuredly, I say to you, he who believes in Me, the works that
> I do he will do also; and greater works than these he will do, because
> I go to My Father.

What could make this seemingly impossible thing come to pass? The coming of the Holy Spirit. You'll recall that a little later, Jesus says, "Nevertheless I tell you the truth. It is to your advantage that I go away; for if I do not go away, the Helper will not come to you; but if I depart, I will send Him to you" (John 16:7).

The Holy Spirit can be everywhere at once and *in* us. It's shocking to contemplate, but Jesus was right. Now we have a much better deal! But it gets even better. As we've seen, the Holy Spirit didn't come empty handed. He came with His arms filled with gifts.

If you need a miracle, He has that. If you need a healing, He has that too. If you need faith, He has that covered. If you need an encouraging message from God, a prophecy, a tongue, or an interpretation—if you need a word of knowledge about your situation, or a word of wisdom, or to discern how the Enemy is attacking you—the Holy Spirit will give these gifts to you and to those around you.

These *charismata,* gifts of grace, are distributed to all who are willing to receive them. And they are for the benefit and blessing of all.

## Summing Up

I know we looked at a lot of Scripture as we explored these nine gifts of the Holy Spirit. But the most important truth to understand is that these manifestations are indeed "of the Holy Spirit."

A loving and good God designed these gifts expressly for our benefit and blessing. What a tragedy that so many of God's children have rejected these gifts. Their rejection grieves the Holy Spirit and hinders the body of Christ.

If you will open yourself up fully to the Holy Spirit, He will give you what you need, when you need it. Ask Him now to manifest His gifts through you "as He wills" for the "profit of all."

# PART 6

# The Language
# of Friendship

# 17

# Why the Controversy?

**M**y dear friend and father in the faith Jack Hayford tells the story of being a young youth pastor attending one of his very first national ministry conferences back in the 1950s. The meeting hosted ministers from a wide variety of denominations from across the country. As he tells it,

> I was young in the ministry, still unoriented to the nuances of interde-
> nominational gatherings, so I wasn't ready for what happened the mo-
> ment I answered a well-known Christian's inquiry following our self-
> introductions. "Jack—It's good to meet you. Where do you minister?"
>
> "I'm in youth ministry with the Foursquare Church."
>
> Sudden silence.
>
> The hand gripping mine went limp as the eyes above a wan
> smile before me turned to find somewhere else in the room to go.
>
> A sudden "Excuse me," and I'm standing there...alone
>
> The bad news is the scenario isn't imagined, but real. The good
> news is that it's far less likely to happen among the broad mix of
> Christ's Body today than when the icy moment slapped my face
> those many years ago.
>
> The memory's pain has long since been handled; the unwitting
> injurer of my soul forgiven, the frequency of such occurrences vastly
> reduced. But the sobering fact is that a peculiar thing happens in
> some people's minds if they know or think you're "one of those,"
> someone who speaks in tongues.*

---

\* Jack W. Hayford, *The Beauty of Spiritual Language* (Nashville: Thomas Nelson, 1996), 53.

I believe one of the great tragedies of the last one hundred years of church history has been the way Satan, the enemy of the church, has successfully made this particular gift so controversial and successfully made huge segments of the body of Christ reluctant to embrace *any* of the empowerments of the Holy Spirit. I know because I was one of them.

You will recall that when I finally opened myself up to receiving a release of the Holy Spirit's power in my life, my initial prayer was something along the lines of, "Okay, Holy Spirit, I want You in my life, I want Your power and Your equipping, but I don't want any of *that* or *that*." One of those *thats* I didn't want was tongues. In other words, I wanted to cherry-pick among the gifts the Holy Spirit brought to me because, deep in my heart, I felt I knew what I needed better than He did.

For reasons that at first may seem mysterious but will become clear a little later on, when it comes to matters of faith, tongues is the thing more people seem to get hung up on than any other. We have seen clearly that it is a gift the Holy Spirit bestows upon God's people for their benefit and for the advancement of His plans and purposes in the world. We have also seen that it is only one of many such gifts. And yet, more than any other gift, precious Christian saints have suffered rejection, scorn, and even persecution because of it.

In this section I hope to blow away the fog of misunderstanding and deception that has hidden the wonderful, empowering truth about this gift from so many for so long.

## The Gift and the Grace

First, it is important to understand the difference between the *gift* of tongues (usually accompanied by the gift of interpretation of tongues) and the *grace* of tongues (often called praying in tongues or praying in the Spirit).

In the previous chapter we saw that "different kinds of tongues" was one of the nine items on the apostle Paul's list of gifts of the Spirit. Two chapters later Paul devotes quite a bit of time to instructing the church at Corinth on how this gift should and should not be expressed in their public worship services. But at the same time he repeatedly encourages them to spend time privately "praying in tongues." Many people get confused because they don't realize Paul is distinguishing between the public gift and the private grace.

He is distinguishing between the gift of tongues that needs to be interpreted and a prayer language, unique to each of us, that we can use as we pray to the Lord. This is why Paul opens 1 Corinthians 14 this way:

> Many **PEOPLE** get **CONFUSED** because they don't realize Paul is **DISTINGUISHING** between the **PUBLIC** gift and the **PRIVATE** grace.

Pursue love, and desire spiritual gifts, but especially that you may prophesy. For he who speaks in a tongue does not speak to men but to God, for no one understands him; however, in the spirit he speaks mysteries. But he who prophesies speaks edification and exhortation and comfort to men. He who speaks in a tongue edifies himself, but he who prophesies edifies the church. I wish you all spoke with tongues, but even more that you prophesied; for he who prophesies is greater than he who speaks with tongues, unless indeed he interprets, that the church may receive edification. (verses 1–5)

Here and throughout the rest of chapter 14, Paul is doing a balancing act. He is attempting to bring correction and order to the way the members of this church are utilizing the *gift* of tongues in their public gatherings, but without discouraging them from yielding to the *grace* of tongues in their private devotional times of prayer.

So on one hand Paul says, in effect, "Concentrate on prophecy in your gatherings because everyone understands it." On the other hand he says, "I wish you all spoke with tongues." We'll look at even more encouragement from Paul along these lines a little later.

As we've seen, the Holy Spirit owns and distributes as He chooses all the nine gifts of the Spirit, including the spiritual gifts of tongues and interpretation of tongues. But I believe everyone is graced with a heavenly prayer language the moment they are baptized in the Holy Spirit (whether they realize it and activate it or not). This is certainly the pattern we see clearly in the book of Acts. Whenever a group of believers receives the outpoured Holy Spirit, we invariably see them speaking with other tongues and prophesying.

As we've seen, this is the sign that so astonishes Peter and his friends when the Holy Spirit falls upon a group of Gentiles:

> While Peter was still speaking these words, the Holy Spirit fell upon all those who heard the word. And those of the circumcision who believed were astonished, as many as came with Peter, because the gift of the Holy Spirit had been poured out on the Gentiles also. *For they heard them speak with tongues and magnify God.* (Acts 10:44–46)

There is really no way to get around this scriptural correlation between the outpouring of the Holy Spirit upon a person and the very visible result of that person's receiving the ability to praise, pray, and prophesy in an unknown tongue.

Nevertheless, this truth has led to what I think is an unfortunate and unhelpful bit of terminology commonly used in Pentecostal and Charismatic circles.

Perhaps you have heard someone speak of receiving the baptism in the Holy Spirit "with the initial evidence of speaking in tongues." For some folks the phrases "baptism in the Holy Spirit" and "with the evidence of speaking in tongues" have been superglued together in their vocabularies. They never say the first phrase without the second one. Other Pentecostals have added an adjective over the years. Now they speak of "the initial *physical* evidence of speaking in tongues."

As I've already pointed out, there is obviously some truth to what they are saying. It's actually the spirit and attitude I hear behind the words to which I really object. It's often used in an argumentative way that I think is ungracious. And the use of the word *evidence* tends to turn what is a beautiful, intimate gift to an individual into something to be judged and evaluated by others.

## A Brief History of Revival

There is some historical background to all of this that would be beneficial for you to know. Back in 1904 there was a great revival in the nation of Wales. It has since come to be known, appropriately enough, as the Welsh Revival. In this remarkable move of God, lukewarm Christians suddenly caught fire for God, churches filled, bars and houses of prostitution closed for lack of business, and most important, more than one hundred thousand people were born again. It all began with some dedicated people praying for an outpouring of the Holy Spirit. And throughout all of it, extraordinary super-natural events similar to those recorded in the book of Acts were reported.

Like seeds that blow in the wind and take root far away from the original plant, that spirit of revival crossed the Atlantic and sprang up in several places in the United States—particularly among a little group of dedicated prayer warriors meeting in a house on Bonnie Brae Avenue near downtown Los Angeles in 1906. The people there had been praying for God to move in power in America as He had moved in Wales. Soon these people of prayer began to experience the book of Acts in their gatherings—particularly various people speaking in tongues and prophesying. The numbers in attendance swelled, and eventually the meetings were moved to an abandoned Methodist church a few blocks away on Azusa Street. Soon thousands were coming and being touched by God in remarkable ways.

> THOUSANDS were coming and being TOUCHED by God in REMARKABLE ways.

The outpouring there came to be known as the Azusa Street Revival, and it is no exaggeration to say that it changed the course of Christianity in America and throughout the world. Many individuals who came from across the country to the Azusa Street meetings experienced the baptism in the Holy Spirit and took that spark back to their home churches.

Entire denominations were eventually birthed out of this move of God, including the Assemblies of God that now has a worldwide membership

numbering more than sixty million in 212 nations. By the way, some esti-
mate the number of Charismatics, Neo-Charismatics, and Pentecostals to
now exceed five hundred million people worldwide, making them second
only to Roman Catholics in size. And Charismatics are by far the fastest
growing of all faith groups on the planet.

The spiritual DNA of all of this can be traced back to what God did in
a few nondescript places back in the early years of the twentieth century. Of
course as soon as the move started changing lives in a major way, there came
the inevitable backlash and counterattack.

Many believers who experienced this beneficial, very biblical release of
the Holy Spirit in their lives found themselves criticized and ostracized for it.
Then, as now, there were many well-meaning Christians too bound up in
religious tradition to acknowledge that God was behind this and that the
obvious fruit it was producing in the lives of others was good.

Of course, no Christian is immune to the temptation to turn something
that has the life and breath of God on it into lifeless religion. And within a
generation, religion began to seep into some aspects of the Pentecostal movement. Some who had been offended by the persecution they received, because of the gift of speaking in tongues
or the grace of prayer language, responded by elevating these manifestations to a place the Holy Spirit never
intended them to have in our theology.
The result was a rigid obsession with
"the initial evidence of speaking in
tongues" as being the only valid indicator of Holy Spirit baptism.

> No Christian is **IMMUNE** to the **TEMPTATION** to turn something that has the **LIFE** and breath of God on it into **LIFELESS** religion.

Consequently, many started put-
ting pressure on people to produce the "evidence" that they had achieved this
special spiritual plateau. For many, tongues became a demand rather than a
desire. For others it became an award proudly achieved rather than a gift
humbly received. The ability to "pray in the Spirit" or to deliver an encouraging message in tongues is a wonderful blessing to the individual believer and

to the body of Christ, respectively. The first spiritually strengthens the individual. The second encourages the church. But both are available to even the most immature new believer who has received the fullness of the Holy Spirit. And they are only two of many possible ways the Holy Spirit wants to work in and through us. Thus they should never be a source of religious pride nor elevated above other spiritual gifts.

One of the elders who serves at the church I pastor tells of how his Pentecostal grandfather wanted desperately for his grandsons to receive the baptism in the Holy Spirit. That is an understandable and honorable desire for a grandfather, because it is such a wonderful blessing to receive. But because of the religious tradition this man was raised in, he was convinced that if he didn't hear his grandsons speak in tongues, they didn't have "it."

One day he had them kneeling at the altar of his church "tarrying" for the Holy Spirit to fall upon them. After a long period of time, my friend realized that he wasn't going to be allowed to get up and get on with his life until his grandfather heard him speak in tongues. As it happened, he and his parents had lived in Japan for several years doing missionary work, and he had learned quite a few phrases in Japanese. So he faked it. He got a very intense, strained look on his face and then began reciting a string of Japanese phrases he knew.

It almost worked. His grandfather bought the act and was rejoicing that his grandson had "broken through." However, his father, who was fluent in Japanese, happened to be listening in and called him on it. He got in trouble for trying to trick his grandfather.

The point is, at some point along the line for many people like my friend's grandfather, the baptism in the Holy Spirit became something one somehow laid hold of through patience, effort, and sacrifice. And in their minds, speaking in tongues was the prize and the only acceptable proof that it had taken place.

> **FRIENDSHIP** with the Holy Spirit is **NOT** that **HARD**.

Perhaps you experienced something akin to that mentality in a previous encounter with Pentecostalism. If so, I'm sorry. Friendship with the

# The Word and the Language

Christians are and should be "people of the Book." The Bible is our first and final authority on all things relating to life and belief. That is why I have filled the pages of this book with Scripture references.

If I make an assertion that can't be backed up with Scripture, you shouldn't accept it as truth. But by the same token, if I point to a truth in the Bible, you shouldn't dismiss it, even if it runs contrary to long-held beliefs or assumptions.

In previous chapters we have already examined a number of scriptures in which the apostle Paul, illuminated and guided by the Holy Spirit, writes about the spiritual gift of tongues (and interpretation of tongues) as well as a similar but distinct grace of tongues that he refers to as praying in the Spirit.

It is this latter topic about which I want you to have a fuller, deeper understanding. Why? Because it will revolutionize your prayer life and help you in countless ways. And based upon what I said above, we should start by assuring ourselves that it is fully scriptural.

## Praying in the Spirit

Let's return to the now-familiar words of 1 Corinthians 14:

> For he who speaks in a tongue does not speak to men but to God, for no one understands him; however, *in the spirit* he speaks mysteries. (verse 2)

Please take note of the phrase I emphasized in the verse above, "in the spirit." These are significant words that Paul will use several times throughout this chapter, as will other New Testament writers in other scriptures we'll examine shortly.

> The **NATURAL** realm and the spiritual **REALM EXIST** side by side, and we **INTERACT** with **BOTH** every day.

As the context of other verses will confirm, the phrase "in the spirit" refers to the spiritual realm as opposed to the physical, natural realm. Most people live their lives believing that the only things that are real are the things they can perceive with their five natural senses. If they can't see it, hear it, touch it, taste it, or smell it, they don't believe it exists. But Jesus taught us there was an invisible realm that is actually more real than the one in which we live—the realm of the spirit. "Some Pharisees asked Jesus when God's kingdom would come. He answered, 'God's kingdom isn't something you can see'" (Luke 17:20, CEV). Paul puts it this way:

> We do not look at the things which are seen, but at the things which are not seen. For the things which are seen are temporary, but the things which are not seen are eternal. (2 Corinthians 4:18)

The natural realm and the spiritual realm exist side by side, and we interact with both every day. It's just that we tend to be much more aware of one than the other.

In 1 Corinthians 14:2, Paul gives us several key pieces of information. Yes, he tells us that speaking in tongues is speaking mysteries, or hidden things, in the Spirit. But before that he tells us that a person who speaks in tongues isn't speaking to people (in this natural realm) but to God (in the spiritual realm).

Now what is a common term we use to describe "speaking to God"? *Prayer!* Prayer is simply speaking to God. And anyone who speaks to God is praying. That's pretty elementary. It also explains why Paul is telling the

Corinthian church that their public worship services aren't the place for exercising this gift. If a person stands up and delivers a long prayer in tongues, no one but the person praying is helped. But if the same person stands up and delivers prophetic encouragement in the native language of everyone gathered, then everyone walks away encouraged.

This is a pretty simple concept to grasp, but just to make sure these Corinthian folks get his point, Paul uses another analogy—musical instruments:

> But now, brethren, if I come to you speaking with tongues, what shall I profit you unless I speak to you either by revelation, by knowledge, by prophesying, or by teaching? Even things without life, whether flute or harp, when they make a sound, unless they make a distinction in the sounds, how will it be known what is piped or played? For if the trumpet makes an uncertain sound, who will prepare for battle? So likewise you, unless you utter by the tongue words easy to understand, how will it be known what is spoken? For you will be speaking into the air. (verses 6–9)

> Paul is **TELLING** the Corinthian **CHURCH** that their public worship **SERVICES** aren't the place for **EXERCISING** this **GIFT**.

Paul is working very hard here to make sure they understand that the gift of tongues and the grace of praying in the Spirit have very important roles to play in the life of a believer, but that creating uninterpreted chaos at public worship services that completely freaks out visitors isn't one of them.

He sums all this up farther down in the chapter when he writes:

> Let all things be done for edification. If anyone speaks in a tongue, let there be two or at the most three, each in turn, and let one

interpret. But if there is no interpreter, let him keep silent in church, and let him speak to himself and to God.... For God is not the author of confusion but of peace. (verses 26–28, 33)

## THE TRUE ROLE OF PRAYER LANGUAGE

Squeezed in between all this corrective instruction for the believers at Corinth are some wonderful insights for us about the true role and purpose of prayer language. Look, for example, at 1 Corinthians 14:14 where Paul says, "For if I pray in a tongue, my spirit prays, but my understanding is unfruitful."

There are three packets of powerful spiritual truth in that little verse. Let's break it down:

1. If I *pray* in a tongue,
2. my *spirit* prays,
3. but my *understanding* (mind) is unfruitful.

This confirms that we can indeed "pray" in tongues, which is why it is so often referred to as a prayer language.

Notice also that when you pray in an unknown tongue, it is your "spirit" that prays. You will recall that early in our journey we learned that we are all three-part beings, comprised of spirit, soul, and body. More specifically, you *are* a spirit, you *have* a soul, and you *live in* a body.

Obviously, it is possible to pray from your soul (mind) because you do it all the time. You think of something you want to tell God, and then you speak it out in prayer. But here we learn that there is a way to pray that bypasses your mind ("my understanding is unfruitful") and in which it is your born-again spirit, made alive by and infused with the Holy Spirit, that prays.

Paul follows this verse with a rhetorical question: "What is the conclusion then?" (verse 15). He essentially says, "So what is the logical thing to do based upon this information?" He then answers his own question: "I will pray with the spirit, and I will also pray with the understanding. I will sing with the spirit, and I will also sing with the understanding" (verse 15).

Praying "with the spirit" clearly refers to praying in tongues, because in the preceding verse Paul says, "If I pray in a tongue, my spirit prays, but my understanding is unfruitful."

Here God's Word is giving us a clear, unambiguous instruction on having a balanced prayer and devotional life. Pray with the spirit *and* pray with the understanding. In your times of private worship, sing with the spirit *and* sing with the understanding.

Are you beginning to see that receiving and using prayer language is scriptural? Paul says bluntly, "I wish you all spoke with tongues" (verse 5). After this exhortation to use tongues liberally in private prayer and private worship, Paul shifts back to giving instruction about using the gift in a public setting:

> God's **WORD** is giving us a clear, **UNAMBIGUOUS** instruction on having a **BALANCED** prayer and devotional **LIFE.**

> I thank my God I speak with tongues more than you all; yet in the
> church I would rather speak five words with my understanding, that
> I may teach others also, than ten thousand words in a tongue. (verses
> 18–19)

Think about it. The greatest apostle of the faith who ever lived prayed in tongues "more than you all." (Paul was obviously from the South of Israel because he said "y'all"!) The man of God who was used by the Holy Spirit to write one-third of the New Testament—that's a lot more than you or I wrote, incidentally—said, "I thank God that I utilize this privilege of grace more than any of you."

# 19

# Beneficial Language

I've already admitted to you that I first approached a relationship with the Holy Spirit as if the gift of tongues was some sort of bitter pill I had to swallow in order to gain the other "good" benefits of having the Holy Spirit as a helper in life. How clueless I was.

I now know what I didn't know then. That is, of the many varieties of blessing and help that come with being baptized in the Holy Spirit, the gift of a prayer language is one of the most wonderful. The very thing I was most wary of has become an indispensable and treasured part of my life and ministry. Let me show you why.

## EDIFYING YOURSELF AND THE CHURCH

It seems that when tongues is the topic, all roads lead to 1 Corinthians 14. Let's revisit this chapter to identify one of the key benefits of praying in the Spirit. You will recall that verse 4 says, "He who speaks in a tongue edifies himself, but he who prophesies edifies the church."

As you probably know, *edify* means "to build up, strengthen, or improve." In other words, when you pray in tongues, you are strengthening yourself spiritually. And when you publicly deliver a word from the Lord in a language everyone understands, you are strengthening the church spiritually.

Keep in mind that Paul is trying to coach and instruct the Corinthian church on the difference between private and public use of spiritual gifts.

Note also the conjunction Paul uses to connect the two thoughts. In most English translations of this verse, the Greek word *de* is translated "but"—as in the verse we just read ("*but* he who prophesies"). However, this word can also be translated "and" or "yet." Indeed, of the 2,870 times the word *de* appears in the Greek New Testament, in many cases it is translated "and." Some of the modern paraphrases use the phrase "on the other hand" to communicate the correct meaning.

Why am I spending so much time explaining a grammatical fine point? Because many people have tried to read too much meaning into that little "but." When they read, "He who speaks in a tongue edifies himself, *but* he who prophesies edifies the church," they interpret Paul to be saying, "Don't speak in tongues. Prophesy instead." (Oddly enough, the vast majority of the folks who make this case don't believe in prophesying either.)

A less confusing translation of this verse then would be, "He who speaks in tongues edifies himself. *On the other hand,* he who prophesies edifies the church."

Other skeptics claim this verse suggests that praying in tongues is somehow a selfish act, and therefore to be avoided. "After all," they say, "Paul says when you pray in tongues, you're just building yourself up."

My response to that argument is always the same: "So?"

What, exactly, is wrong with growing stronger spiritually? Isn't that why we encourage new Christians to read their Bibles every day? I've found that spending time with God daily builds me up as well. Should this be avoided? Is there some virtue in being spiritually weak and defeated that I'm not aware of?

> **WHAT**, exactly, is **WRONG** with **GROWING** stronger **SPIRITUALLY**?

Yes, when you pray in tongues, or in the Spirit, you build yourself up. And being built up is vital if we're going to be useful, productive, victorious citizens in God's kingdom. It is also true that in a public worship gathering, your focus should be on building up the body as a whole. By the way, I've found that I'm not much help to others unless I've first built myself up. If I don't obtain some spiritual supply in my prayer closet, I don't have much to give when I walk into a gathering of believers.

Obviously, there's nothing wrong with building yourself up. In fact, Paul goes to great lengths throughout the rest of the chapter to ensure that his readers understand that. He repeatedly emphasizes his wish that they all speak in tongues and affirms that he speaks in tongues more than any of them.

As a matter of fact, before Paul closes out this chapter, he seems concerned that the leaders of the church might have gotten the wrong impression. So, in verse 39 he adds, "And do not forbid to speak with tongues." Paul seems to realize that just because something good and helpful can potentially be abused, there will be people who will try to throw the baby out with the bath water. And he is right. I've heard pastors and religious leaders directly disobey this verse. They have forbidden anyone under their ministry to speak in tongues.

The fact is, every good gift and practice in the church can be abused or misused. But we shouldn't make the potential for misuse an excuse for robbing ourselves of the gift altogether.

## A VITAL PIECE OF ARMOR

What many people don't realize is that the Word points to praying in the Spirit as being a vital part of the "armor of God." Most believers are very familiar with the list in Ephesians 6 of "the whole armor of God." In fact, twice Paul uses the word *whole* in conjunction with this list of spiritual defenses and weapons.

We just learned that praying in the Spirit builds us up or makes us strong. Correct? Now notice how Paul introduces his description of the armor of God:

> Finally, my brethren, *be strong in the Lord* and in the power of His
> might. Put on the whole armor of God, that you may be able to stand
> against the wiles of the devil. For we do not wrestle against flesh and
> blood, but against principalities, against powers, against the rulers of

the darkness of this age, against spiritual hosts of wickedness in the heavenly places. Therefore take up the whole armor of God, that you may be able to withstand in the evil day, and having done all, to stand. (Ephesians 6:10–13)

This entire passage involves instruction on how to "be strong in the Lord and in the power of His might." Why do we need supernatural spiritual strength? Because we're in a daily battle with "the devil"—and against "principalities, against powers, against the rulers of the darkness of this age, against spiritual hosts of wickedness in the heavenly places." Now ask yourself, is that really a battle you want to go into weak, depleted, and defenseless?

> As you **LOOK** around at the **ENCROACHING** spiritual **DARKNESS** in our **CULTURE** and in the world, don't we **NEED** all the spiritual **STRENGTH** we can get?

Paul also says we need to have "His might" so we can be able to "withstand in the evil day." Is it possible that we're in an evil day right now? As you look around at the encroaching spiritual darkness in our culture and in the world, don't we need all the spiritual strength we can get?

Paul goes on to show us how to stand in strength. He begins by listing the familiar items of spiritual armor:

Stand therefore, having girded your waist with truth, having put on the breastplate of righteousness, and having shod your feet with the preparation of the gospel of peace; above all, taking the shield of faith with which you will be able to quench all the fiery darts of the wicked one. And take the helmet of salvation, and the sword of the Spirit, which is the word of God;... (verses 14–17)

Now that is where most people who quote this passage stop. They mention the "sword of the Spirit" and then quit. But please notice the absence of a period after the word "God" in that last verse. That semicolon tells us the sentence continues. Why is it that we never keep reading beyond that point? The sentence continues, "…praying always with all prayer and supplication *in the Spirit*" (verse 18).

Have you ever been taught that praying in the Spirit is a part of your spiritual armor? It is. And once you understand that praying in the Spirit builds you up spiritually, it makes perfect sense that Paul would mention it in a passage in which he's teaching us how to "be strong in the Lord."

## THE WHOLE ARMOR OF GOD

You and I need the "whole" armor of God—not just a few pieces of it. We have an enemy who comes only "to steal, and to kill, and to destroy" (John 10:10). Our adversary "walks about like a roaring lion, seeking whom he may devour" (1 Peter 5:8).

Yes, we need the sword of the Spirit—the Word of God. When the Enemy tempts Jesus in the wilderness, Jesus repulses the attacks by quoting the Scriptures. "It is written…," Jesus says repeatedly. Furthermore, the Word is the standard against which we must measure every prophetic word and assertion by man. If it doesn't line up with the Word, don't accept it.

Yes, we need our waists girded with truth, the breastplate of righteousness, and all the rest of it. But we're missing something vital unless we are "praying always with all prayer and supplication *in the Spirit*." It is the source of your strength to stand and of your power to fight.

## BUILDING YOURSELF UP

Is there another scriptural witness who can testify that praying in the Spirit builds us up spiritually? Yes! Take a look at the one-chapter book of Jude. There we find, "But you, beloved, building yourselves up on your most holy faith, praying in the Holy Spirit" (verse 20).

What is Jude's prescription for a stronger faith and for building ourselves up? "Praying in the Holy Spirit."

More than two decades ago—before I opened myself to the baptism in the Holy Spirit—I was preaching a series of revival services in one of the fastest-growing churches in the Southern Baptist Convention. In fact, this church was one of the denomination's leading churches in baptisms. I was excited to spend some time with the pastor because God was obviously doing some exciting things at that church and I wanted to find out why. This man also had a reputation for being a great soul-winner personally, and that was something I had a passion for as well.

> "To be honest, I **NEED** all the **BUILDING UP** I can get."

At a certain point in my time there, I learned from a third party, to my great surprise, that this pastor had received the baptism in the Holy Spirit and consistently prayed in tongues in his times alone with God. Based on the prejudices and misconceptions I held at the time, I found that a little alarming.

Eventually, I worked up the nerve to ask him about it. "I hear that you pray in tongues," I queried when we were alone.

He nodded and said, "Yes."

"Can I ask you why?" I followed up.

He looked at me and very matter-of-factly said, "Well, the Bible says it builds you up. And to be honest, I need all the building up I can get."

At that point our conversation was interrupted and we moved on to other topics. But I've thought about his simple, humble response many times since that day. As the scriptures we have examined in this chapter make clear, he was right. The Bible does tell us praying in the Spirit builds us up. And we could *all* use every bit of spiritual strengthening we can get—especially in the days in which we're living.

Please ask yourself, *If the Bible says praying in tongues builds me up, why would I not want that?*

20

# The Choice Is Yours

As a pastor, it has been my privilege to lead many believers—after opening the Word and showing them the things we have been exploring in this book—into receiving the baptism in the Holy Spirit. And after many years of helping other Christians make the same wonderful discovery I did, I have noticed some common misconceptions and fallacies in the thinking of those who seem to struggle with receiving their prayer language.

One of the most prevalent is the assumption that once you're open to receiving your prayer language, it will somehow just involuntarily come gushing out of you like an open fire hydrant of foreign words. I understand. I used to think something like that too.

Many people seem to think that praying in tongues for the first time will be immediately followed by falling into a trance and convulsing bodily a couple of times.

Well, no.

What's even worse, because of this same misconception, many people who might otherwise be open to receiving the grace of a prayer language are fearful of it because they don't want to be in the checkout line at the grocery store and suddenly start uncontrollably delivering a message in tongues. They imagine how mortified they would be if the Holy Spirit were to choose the exact moment of a big business presentation to suddenly have them belt out a song in a heavenly version of Swahili.

Again, no.

Nothing about the gifts of the Holy Spirit works that way. The fact is, operating in any of the spiritual gifts is a choice you make. Recall Paul's simple summing up of all he'd written about tongues in 1 Corinthians 14. He says, "What is the conclusion then? I will pray with the spirit, and I will also pray with the understanding. I will sing with the spirit, and I will also sing with the understanding" (verse 15).

Notice the four appearances of the word "will" in the verse above. This makes it clear that you have to exercise your will to pray or sing in the Spirit just as you do when you pray or sing with your understanding. In other words, it's a choice. It's like anything else we do in our Christian lives. We have to yield to the Holy Spirit. We have to choose to cooperate with Him.

## An Exercise of Faith

Another common fallacy is that stepping out and praying in tongues won't require any faith. The fact is, it requires a big step of faith. But then so does regular prayer in your native language.

Think about it. You're in a room all by yourself and you choose to start talking out loud to a God you've never seen. If someone happens to walk by your door, they might ask, "Who is that person talking to all alone in there?"

All prayer is a step of faith. That's the core of the message in the familiar words of Hebrews 11:6: "But without faith it is impossible to please Him, for he who comes to God must believe that He is, and that He is a rewarder of those who diligently seek Him."

> All **PRAYER** is a step of **FAITH**.

Often when we pray, we don't *feel* a thing. It can sometimes seem that our prayers are getting no higher than the ceiling. But if we know the Word, we know—by faith—that God hears our prayers and that He draws near to those who draw near to Him.

In the same way, stepping out in your prayer language is a faith exercise. I have heard some people who are brand new in all of this say, "I've tried and it just sounds like a few syllables of gibberish to me." Well, that shouldn't surprise us. If you're a parent, think about what it sounded like when your children first started learning to talk. They didn't wake up one day and start speaking in fully formed, complex sentences. All children start with a few halting syllables.

When my grandson was about eighteen months old, he was over for a visit, toddling around, and pointing at me, saying, "Ma-pa-da-de-ma-pa-ta-ya." He seemed quite earnest about what he was communicating, so I said, "Really?" And he immediately replied, "Ma-pa-da-de-ma-pa-ta-ya." We carried on quite a conversation there for a while, though I didn't understand a word he said. Apparently I didn't have the gift of interpretation. However, his mother did. He would rattle off a few unintelligible syllables, and she seemed to know exactly what he wanted.

When my youngest son was a toddler and was beginning to talk, I remember being at the dinner table and hearing him, from his high chair, say something that sounded like, "Ba-ga-ba-ba!" He was clearly trying to tell us something, but his mother and I had no clue what it was. Then he would repeat it even louder and more emphatically, "Ba-ga-ba-ba!"

Then his older brother, who was four or five years old at the time, would say, "He wants some more corn." We would look at him and wonder, *How on earth did you get "More corn" out of "Ba-ga-ba-ba"?* But, sure enough, we would put some more corn on his plate and he would get a big smile on his face and be thrilled.

My point is, once you pray for and receive the baptism in the Holy Spirit, you may not have a fully formed vocabulary with complex syntax the first time you step out by faith and express your prayer language. But you might. I have certainly known people who experienced that, but it is not the norm. Nor will your prayer language necessarily be an actual language spoken by some nation or tribe of people on earth. Note what Paul said in the first verse of the "love chapter," 1 Corinthians 13: "Though I speak with the tongues of men and of angels..." Your prayer language might be an angelic tongue. Nevertheless, I have heard many testimonies of people who delivered a message in tongues in a group of believers only to have a stranger from another country come up to them afterward and say, "You were speaking my native language and in the perfect regional dialect of my home. You even had the accent!"

Getting started is a choice that requires faith. As I said above, the Holy Spirit is not going to take control of your vocal chords, lungs, and tongue and speak out for you. Spiritual gifts don't work that way. For example, the Bible talks about a "gift of giving," but no one with that gift has ever had a check jump out of his or her checkbook and fly into the offering plate as it went by.

No, to operate in the gift of giving requires stepping out by faith and choosing, by an act of your conscious will, to write a check. Likewise, if you're going to pray in the Spirit, you're going to have to open your mouth and start talking in a language you don't know. It will require faith and a conscious decision to cooperate with the Holy Spirit.

## A Matter of Trust

Another obstacle frequently keeps people from fully yielding to the Holy Spirit. That barrier boils down to a matter of trust. Allow me to explain.

Over the years I have encountered several people who genuinely wanted to fully and wholly cooperate with the Holy Spirit, but were held back by fear. Specifically, they were afraid that if they totally let down their guard and opened themselves to the Holy Spirit's influence, they might end up being influenced by something dark instead. I'm talking about demonic powers. This has been a concern I've heard on a number of occasions. In fact, I remember having that thought myself. In my heart I wondered, *What if I open my spirit up to the Holy Spirit but somehow get a demon instead?*

The good news is that two thousand years ago Jesus anticipated these fears, and one day He addressed them directly in a conversation with His disciples. Before we examine that conversation, however, we need to look at some earlier words of Jesus that illuminate the later ones.

In Luke 10:19 we hear Jesus speaking to the seventy disciples He's sending out in pairs on special short-term ministry trips. Jesus tells them,

> Behold, I give you the authority to trample on serpents and scorpions,
> and over all the power of the enemy, and nothing shall by any means
> hurt you.

There is a lot of wonderful truth in Jesus's statement. But the one thing I want you to note about it now is that Jesus uses "serpents" and "scorpions" to symbolize demonic powers. He isn't giving them the power to walk on literal snakes and actual stinging arthropods. We can know that "serpents and scorpions" refers to demons, because He follows this up with, "...and over all the power of the enemy." This is further confirmed by the very next verse where Jesus says, "Nevertheless do not rejoice in this, that the spirits are subject to you."

With that in mind, let's jump forward one chapter and look with fresh eyes at something Jesus tells His disciples about prayer:

> So I say to you, ask, and it will be given to you; seek, and you will find; knock, and it will be opened to you. For everyone who asks receives, and he who seeks finds, and to him who knocks it will be opened. If a son asks for bread from any father among you, will he give him a stone? Or if he asks for a fish, will he give him a *serpent* instead of a fish? Or if he asks for an egg, will he offer him a *scorpion*? If you then, being evil, know how to give good gifts to your children, *how much more will your heavenly Father give the Holy Spirit to those who ask Him!* (Luke 11:9–13)

The context of this entire passage is Jesus's answering the disciples' request, "Teach us to pray." After giving them what we call the Lord's Prayer or the Model Prayer, Jesus then offers them (and us) a powerful reminder about the generosity and goodness of God.

"Ask, seek, and knock," Jesus says, "and you will receive, find, and see doors open." More important, Jesus lets us know that when you're asking God for something good and holy, you

> **JESUS** then **OFFERS** them (and us) a powerful **REMINDER** about the generosity and **GOODNESS** of **GOD**.

don't need to be concerned about receiving something unholy or demonic ("a serpent" or "a scorpion"). He's a good Father.

It is Jesus's last sentence above that really clinches it for us where asking for the baptism in the Holy Spirit is concerned: "How much more will your heavenly Father give the Holy Spirit to those who ask Him!"

Do we really think that a loving, compassionate heavenly Father would allow us to receive an unclean, unholy demonic spirit when we are obeying His Word's encouragement to receive the Holy Spirit? Of course not! It's an insult to the goodness, power, and integrity of God. But I had that thought nonetheless. And so do many others.

The cool thing is that more than two thousand years ago, Jesus anticipated that fear and addressed it head on.

## OTHER ASSORTED HANG-UPS

That fear of getting something bad when I was asking for something good wasn't the only obstacle that stood between me and a full release of the Holy Spirit in my life. I had a number of other hang-ups. Actually my wife, Debbie, and I both did. As with everything else in our lives, we walked the journey into the fullness of the Holy Spirit together.

I was in full-time ministry, and we had been hearing about the baptism in the Holy Spirit for several years. We loved the Lord. We loved and honored His Word. And if there was something God had for us—something that would make us more effective for Him—we wanted it. But we had received a lot of negative teaching about the gifts of the Holy Spirit when we were younger. The roots of that religious indoctrination ran pretty deep. And we still weren't convinced from a scriptural standpoint that the baptism in the Holy Spirit was a valid experience after salvation.

For some reason we never questioned the validity of water baptism after salvation. But we had a problem with the whole idea of receiving Holy Spirit baptism after salvation.

We had lots of questions but eventually found ourselves in a church with a pastor who understood many of the things I have shared on the previous pages. He understood and taught the reality of the three baptisms and that the gifts of the Spirit are still very much available to believers today. Not long after we joined that church, the pastor taught a class about these things.

He took us through scripture after scripture, and before he was finished, we were both convinced. We were ready to receive. We walked to the front of the room at the end of the teaching and asked him to lead us in a prayer to receive the baptism in the Holy Spirit.

He laid his hands upon Debbie's head and prayed for her. Then he led her in a prayer of her own. The biblical pattern in the book of Acts is that when the Holy Spirit fell upon individuals and filled them, they often began immediately speaking in tongues. He asked Debbie if any words or syllables were coming up in her awareness. She said yes, and he encouraged her to speak them out. She did so and, on the spot, had the beginnings of her prayer language.

The pastor took me through the same process as well. At the end, the pastor asked, "Do you feel like you want to say something?" Indeed I did. What I felt coming up from my spirit into my conscious mind were not words or syllables from a language I did not know. I felt a message rising up in me. He said, "Just say what's coming to your mind."

I said, "We've got to be a holy people. It's important for God's people to live righteously and with purity."

I didn't know it at the time, but I was prophesying. That was a baby-steps version of a prophetic word. I now know that this fit the biblical pattern too. Acts 19:6 says, "And when Paul had laid hands on them, the Holy Spirit came upon them, and they spoke with tongues and prophesied."

> I could **SENSE** a real **DIFFERENCE** in my **HEART** and in my **PRAYER** times.

In the weeks that followed, I could sense a real difference in my heart and in my prayer times. But I was a little troubled by the fact that I hadn't spoken in tongues. Debbie, on the other hand, was growing and maturing in her prayer language by the day. To be honest, it tweaked my manly pride just a little to have my wife flowing in a blessing from the Holy Spirit that I didn't seem to have.

A couple of months later, Debbie and I were getting ready for church on a Sunday morning when I noticed she had an odd smile on her face. She had the look of a person who knows a fun secret that you don't know. I remember thinking, *What is she grinning about?* When I couldn't stand it any longer, I asked her what she was up to.

I could tell she was reluctant to tell me, and that stirred my curiosity up even more. I pressed her and finally she said, "Well, I don't want to embarrass you."

That was more than I could bear. "What? Embarrass me about what?"

She said, "Okay. Last night I couldn't sleep, so I got up and went into the living room to read my Bible. Later when I came back to the bedroom… well…that's when I heard you."

"That's when you heard me what?" I said, really confused now. "Was I snoring?"

She said, "No. Speaking in tongues."

"What?"

"Yeah, you were speaking in tongues last night in your sleep. Talking and talking like crazy in some other language."

"You're making that up!"

"No, I promise," she told me. "Why would I make that up?"

It seems I had the ability to use my prayer language in my sleep but, at that point, couldn't do so while awake. Here's what I theorized later about that experience. I believe I was so hardheaded that my spirit had to wait until my mind fell asleep before it could pray. My mind was so indoctrinated and bound up in tradition that it was getting in the way. But with my mind shut down during sleep, my born-again spirit finally had the freedom to commune with the Holy Spirit and pray.

> My **MIND** was so **INDOCTRINATED** and bound up in **TRADITION** that it was getting in the **WAY**.

I would later mention that experience to my pastor. His response was, "Oh yeah, that happens with a lot of hardheaded people."

*Well, that's very encouraging,* I remember thinking. *It's good to know I'm not alone!* He went on to say that I had probably just built up a stronghold in my mind against this gift. Perhaps you have as well. Allow me to share the advice my pastor gave me.

He said, "Robert, the next time you are completely alone, have total privacy, and can spend some unhurried time with God, I want you to do the following. Spend a little time reading your Bible, then put on a favorite worship CD and just worship God for a while. Be very unguarded, open, and vocal in your worship. Remember, no one can hear you but your heavenly Father. Then after you've praised, thanked, and worshiped God vocally in your own words for a while, just shift over, open your mouth, and start praying in a language you don't know. Trust God with it and open your mouth in abandonment and speak. Trust Him in this just like you do in everything else."

I couldn't wait to follow his recommendation and did so at my first opportunity. I was hopeful. I figured that if I had the gift of tongues in my sleep, I must have it down in there somewhere while awake too. Indeed, I began speaking in my heavenly prayer language from that day forward. And yet it was a little anticlimactic. I suppose I expected to feel electric tingles running through my limbs or see visions of angels on ladders or something. To be honest, I didn't "feel" anything.

## Faith More than Feelings

The next time I saw my pastor, he asked me if I'd had a breakthrough. I told him I had but that I was surprised about the lack of fireworks. He reassured me, saying, "Don't worry about that, Robert. Just keep doing it in faith. You probably don't feel anything when you tithe either. But you do it in faith, obedience, and expectancy anyway. Just keep on." So I did.

A few months later I found myself away from home on a ministry trip. I was staying in a hotel and rose early in the morning to walk, pray, and spend some time with the Lord. I eventually found myself beside the deserted swimming pool in the hotel's courtyard.

There was a bit of a chill in the air, and I knew I wasn't likely to be interrupted. So I just began to walk around that swimming pool praising

God and praying. As I prayed in English, I felt something I'd rarely, if ever, felt before. I sensed a weight and power on my prayers as if the Holy Spirit Himself were carrying them to the Father.

> It was **EVIDENT** to me that my **BORN-AGAIN** human **SPIRIT** and the Holy Spirit were in **SYNC**.

Then I had a thought that I now know didn't originate with me. I heard, *You ought to pray in the Spirit.*

I obeyed that prompting, and I'm so glad I did. I began speaking in my prayer language, and almost instantly it just…took off. That's the only way I know to describe it. It was different. It was a language. I still had complete control of it and could have stopped at any instant, but I didn't want to. There was such a beautiful flow to it—it was evident to me that my born-again human spirit and the Holy Spirit were in sync.

I recall that I began to pace back and forth beside that pool as if I was preaching on the platform of a church. It felt appropriate to gesture as I spoke in this language I didn't understand. I suppose that if someone had peeked in on me in that moment, they might have thought I had been up all night drinking. But that is precisely what some of those in the Jerusalem crowd on the Day of Pentecost thought about the disciples.

I didn't know what I was saying, because at that point I did not know to ask the Holy Spirit for the interpretation. But I knew I was doing some mighty preaching, declaring, and prophesying. And I knew it was doing some good for the kingdom of God. I remember thinking, *Ahhh,* this *is what they're talking about! This is what they call the anointing.*

What was I doing? I was praying *in* the Spirit.

From that moment forward I knew what Paul meant when he told the believers in Corinth, "I wish you all spoke with tongues" (1 Corinthians 14:5).

I wish it for you. Why? Because as we've seen, it is thoroughly *scriptural* and it is an extraordinary *benefit.* But you will not receive it unless you open yourself in trust and yieldedness. Why? Because it is also a *choice.*

## SUMMING UP

Are you like I was? Has tradition or bad teaching in your past created strongholds in your mind and heart that keep you from opening yourself to all the Holy Spirit wants to do in you? If so, you are also limiting what He can do *through* you.

Are there some barriers standing between you and a full release of the Holy Spirit's power and influence in your life? If so, why would you allow them to remain? I can assure you, if you had even an inkling of how wonderful it is to have the voice and guidance of the Holy Spirit in full dimension, you wouldn't hesitate for a moment.

Have you been afraid that if you drop your spiritual defenses, you might be opening yourself to influence by something unclean or unholy? Now you know you can rest in the promise that comes from the lips of Jesus Himself:

If a son asks for bread from any father among you, will he give him a stone? Or if he asks for a fish, will he give him a serpent instead of a fish? Or if he asks for an egg, will he offer him a scorpion? If you then, being evil, know how to give good gifts to your children, how much more will your heavenly Father give the Holy Spirit to those who ask Him! (Luke 11:11–13)

You can trust Him. As James tells us, "Every good gift and every perfect gift is from above, and comes down from the Father of lights, with whom there is no variation or shadow of turning" (1:17). If there ever was a good and perfect gift that came down from the Father, the Holy Spirit is that gift. He is good. He is perfect.

What are you waiting for?

PART 7

# The God You Need
## to Know

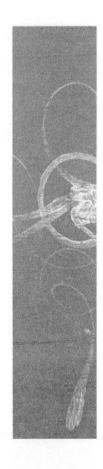

# Your New Best Friend

A story is told of a poor man in Eastern Europe in the early nineteen hundreds. The man longed to move himself and his family to the United States in hopes of building a better life. After several years of scrimping and saving, he finally accumulated enough money to purchase a third-class ticket on a large steamship to New York City.

He only had enough money for one ticket. So he and his wife decided he would go ahead of his family, find a job, and as quickly as possible save enough money to bring them all to America to join him.

He spent virtually all his savings on the ticket, leaving him very little for purchasing food on board the ship. Plus, he would need what little money he had left in order to get established once he got to the promised land of America. So he bought a wheel of hard cheese and box of crackers to keep him sustained on the twelve-day voyage to the New World.

As his ocean journey began, he carefully rationed his cheese and crackers, making sure he would have enough to carry him through the whole trip. Sometimes during mealtimes, he would look longingly through the windows of the dining rooms where simple but hearty and abundant meals were being served to other passengers. The food looked wonderful, but he comforted himself in the knowledge that on some future day he would be earning enough money to eat well and feed his family. Then he would slip back to his little stateroom for his ration of cheese.

On the final day of the journey, there was great excitement on board because soon the Statue of Liberty and the Ellis Island entry point for new immigrants would be in sight. It was a good thing, too, because the man had eaten his final portion of molding cheese and stale crackers at noon the previous day. He was hungry.

The man eventually found himself at the railing of the ship, standing beside one of the ship's stewards. They conversed a bit about the excitement of the arrival. Then the steward asked a question. "I don't mean to pry, sir. But I noticed that you didn't take any of your meals with your fellow passengers in the dining hall. I trust we didn't do anything to offend you."

"Oh my goodness, no," the man said. "Everyone has been so gracious. It's just that I am saving what little money I have left for my expenses getting established in America. I didn't want to spend money on food."

> The **OPPORTUNITY** for blessing and **PROVISION** on his **JOURNEY** had been forever **MISSED**.

The steward's expression of confusion became one of shock and dismay when the meaning of the man's words sank in. "Oh, my dear friend!" the steward said. "Did you not know that three meals each day were included in the price of your ticket? We set a place for you at every meal, but you never came!"

Of course, the man didn't know, until it was too late—and the opportunity for blessing and provision on his journey had been forever missed.

## A Place Set for Us

Every day I encounter Christians who are just like this man. They live without the blessing and provision available to them as born-again children of God on the journey of life. Jesus sent the Holy Spirit as a wonderful gift—a gift better than having Jesus Himself with us—and the price for His presence in our lives was fully purchased by Jesus on the cross. The Holy Spirit came with all the other amazing blessings of salvation. But some believers never receive and unwrap the gift.

Instead, they live lives of cheese-and-crackers Christianity. They muddle through this world powerless and deprived of the richness of God's presence, consoling themselves with the knowledge that heaven awaits by and by.

Some look longingly at the power and usefulness in God's kingdom that others seem to enjoy. Their noses pressed against the window, they see certain believers who obviously hear the voice of God clearly and seem to always be blessing others with timely messages of encouragement and spiritual refreshing. These are the same Christians who consistently seem to make wise choices and avoid pitfalls, almost as if they know in advance what lies around the corner. They pray with a higher dimension of power and effectiveness. Miracles and amazing "coincidences" are a part of these believers' daily lives.

Those on the outside assume such privileges are for a special class of Christian, not them. But they are wrong. God has set a place for them at the bountiful banquet table of His Holy Spirit. But they never come.

## AVAILABLE TO ALL

Baptism in the Holy Spirit is available to every believer. He is not a merit badge or a medal earned by an elite few. He is not a level of spirituality achieved through effort or time. He is a gift freely poured out upon those who will ask and receive, even the newest young believer. As Jesus says, "If you then, being evil, know how to give good gifts to your children, how much more will your heavenly Father give the Holy Spirit to those who ask Him!" (Luke 11:13).

Some other Christians simply don't know what they've been missing. They assume cheese-and-crackers Christianity is all that's available. Perhaps you were one of those before you picked up this book. By now you know that is not the case.

By way of reminder, here are just a few of the benefits and blessings friendship with the Holy Spirit brings:

- *Comfort.* Jesus called the Holy Spirit the Comforter, and He is a constant presence in our lives, ready and able to infuse us with peace and assurance (John 14:15–17; 1 Corinthians 14:3).
- *Conviction.* One of the Holy Spirit's roles is to convict us that we need God and to show us that we are separated from Him. Then

He draws us to Jesus, the only answer to that need, and finally convinces us that we have been put in right standing with God through Him ( John 16:8–11).

- *Counsel.* The Holy Spirit is the Counselor who leads us into all truth and shows us things to come; He enables us to avoid pitfalls, helps us avoid self-inflicted wounds, and gives us the perfect words to say in difficult circumstances ( John 16:13; Acts 16:6).
- *Fellowship.* The Holy Spirit is an ever-present companion and friend who just happens to be God (2 Corinthians 13:14; Philippians 2:1).
- *Gifts.* The Spirit of God comes with gifts specially designed to equip us for maximum usefulness in God's kingdom. When we receive and operate in these gifts, the whole body becomes stronger, healthier, and more fulfilled (Romans 12:6–8; 1 Corinthians 12:1–10; 14:1; Hebrews 2:4).
- *Fruit.* The more the Spirit is free to operate in our lives, the more fruit we tend to bear. If you need more love, peace, patience, kindness, or any other good thing in your life, you simply need to yield more of yourself to the Holy Spirit (Galatians 5:22–23; Ephesians 5:9).
- *Revealed mysteries.* The Holy Spirit is able to bring us insight and understanding unavailable through any other means. This in-cludes revelation of God's plans and purposes as well as helpful knowledge of the keys to solving seemingly unsolvable challenges (1 Corinthians 2:6–12).
- *Prayer help.* The Holy Spirit is ready and available to help us pray more effectively and to actually pray through us. Many Christians find prayer a boring, lifeless exercise, because they never open themselves to this ministry of the Spirit (Romans 8:26; 1 Corin-thians 14:15).
- *Power.* The power to be effective witnesses, to be bold, to under-stand the Bible, and to pretty much do everything the Christian life is supposed to involve comes from the indwelling, baptizing

Holy Spirit (Luke 24:49; Acts 1:8; 10:38; Romans 15:13; 1 Thessalonians 1:5).

- *Liberty.* True freedom is a work of the Holy Spirit in our lives. It's a work we must authorize and cooperate with (Romans 8:2; 2 Corinthians 3:17).

And there's so much more. It's amazing to contemplate all the things the Holy Spirit stands ready to do in the life of the believer. When you do contemplate that reality, it makes it even more incredible that so many Christians continue to say, "No thanks," to His work in their lives.

Some continue to allow fear, misinformation, religious prejudice, or just bad old-fashioned pride to keep them from throwing the door of their hearts wide open to a God who loves them and only wants the best for them.

## RECEIVE THE HOLY SPIRIT

Now that we are at the end of this biblical journey, I pray you're not one of the fearful, prejudiced, or prideful Christians who refuses the astonishing offer of friendship with God Himself. My hope is that you are ready to ask and receive, because I know the need for the Holy Spirit's power and presence in a believer's life is as critical today as it was in the day of the apostles. And experiencing His power and presence really is as simple as just asking and receiving. Our heavenly Father receives joy and pleasure when He gives the Holy Spirit to those who ask.

Just as with the salvation experience, baptism in the Holy Spirit is a free gift from the Father that you can receive by faith.

What can you expect once you do? You can expect things to be different in your life. You may or may not feel anything at the moment you ask and receive. Again, this is similar to the salvation experience; some people feel nothing but move forward by faith, while others experience tears, joy, release, or a host of other physical and emotional impacts. Everyone is unique.

However, the pattern of Scripture is clear. When a person receives the Holy Spirit, there are frequently specific manifestations associated with the encounter. Some become emotional or express a gift of the Holy Spirit such as tongues or prophecy, while others notice a change in their insight on Scripture or boldness to witness. While manifestations aren't required to receive the Holy Spirit, they are common.

The Holy Spirit is
NOT MYSTICAL.
He's PRACTICAL.

The manifestations and gifts are indeed wonderful. They will bless and transform your life in countless ways. But it's not these that I covet for you most of all. More than the gifts the Holy Spirit brings, I want you to know the amazing *person* of the Holy Spirit! Fellowship, communion, and intimacy—in other words, the *friendship*—with the Holy Spirit is the greatest blessing of all.

The Holy Spirit is not mystical. He's practical. He wants to come and help you every day. He wants to be your walk-beside, talk-to-every-moment, comforting, empowering best friend!

My prayer is that you won't spend another day in meager cheese-and-crackers Christianity when a banquet of gifts and empowerments has already been purchased for you. He came with the purchase of your ticket to heaven.

Is the Holy Spirit your best friend? He can be today.

# The God I Never Knew

So that you make the most of each session, this study guide is designed to be used *after* the chapters assigned for each session have been read. Whether you are studying *The God I Never Knew* as an individual or in a group, the goal is for you to think a little more deeply, contemplate and pray about what you are learning, and apply the truths of God's Word to your personal life.

The study guide has eight sessions. However, if your group wants to move more slowly, just adjust the reading assignments and use of questions accordingly.

## READ THE CHAPTERS PRIOR TO EACH SESSION

Each session covers designated chapters of *The God I Never Knew*. As you read the chapters, make notes and highlight passages in the book that speak to, challenge, or apply to you personally. In your reading and reflection, ask the Lord to reveal insights so that when you come to the study-guide section, you will be equipped to benefit the most from the questions.

## INTRODUCTION AND GENERAL FEEDBACK

At the start of each group session, ask about answers or updates to prayer from prior sessions. Then spend some time in prayer together. Next have someone read the brief introduction aloud to remind everyone of the focus of the discussion. The leader should then invite the group to share any questions, concerns, "ahas," insights, or comments arising from their personal time with the material.

## No Fear

*The God I Never Knew* is about the wonderful person and ministry of the Holy Spirit in the life of the believer. As you might imagine (and as the author readily admits in his personal testimony), it's possible that your group members represent a variety of backgrounds and teaching about the Holy Spirit. That's okay! There are only three prerequisites for group participation: (1) a humble desire to grow in Christ and learn from His Word, (2) hearts and minds truly open to what God may reveal through the author's insights into His Word, and (3) a commitment to interact gently and respectfully with one another and with the material presented.

Group facilitators and participants need not be afraid of the topic or of differences of opinion. A healthy approach for handling disagreements or concepts that may be new to someone is to say, "Let's see what God's Word has to say," and then review the pertinent scriptures referenced by the author. If after discussion it's obvious that a participant continues to struggle with a concept, consider moving on by saying, "Let's agree to take this concept to the Lord in prayer this week and report back, okay?" This will not only help keep discussions calm and on-target, but it will also help the group refocus on the Bible as the final word on an issue.

Above all, there should never be any pressure or browbeating for others to see things in a certain way. You're on a journey of discovery together. Gentleness is the key—trusting the Holy Spirit to reveal truth and, if necessary, change hearts and minds. You just never know: the heart or mind He changes might be your own!

## Go Through the Questions

The reflection and discussion questions are designed to focus on how each person relates to the main topics of the chapters. Most questions are designed to serve the group and encourage discussion, not to elicit a particular answer. With that mind, *don't race through the questions.* Take your time and allow the Holy Spirit to work. It isn't necessary to go around the circle before moving on to the next question. The best discussions occur when people feel free to speak into the discussion. Group discussions are actually opportunities for God's Spirit to minister uniquely through one believer to another in very specific ways. If you don't get through all the questions for a session, no worries. Relax and trust God to take the discussion where He wants to take it.

## KEY VERSES

Each session offers a theme verse that connects to the session's content. Groups should read the verse out loud, and if someone in the group has a different Bible translation, ask him or her to read it aloud so the group can get a bigger picture of the meaning of the passage. Encourage participants to memorize these verses to enrich their understanding and appreciation of the personal ministry of God the Holy Spirit.

## CLOSE EACH SESSION IN PRAYER

Praying together is the most powerful way to make your discussion effective, authentic, and relevant. Do not leave too little time for prayer! Be sure group members have opportunity to share their requests. In several of the sessions, we also suggest that you begin the prayer time with a few minutes of silent prayer, in which each participant can talk with God personally regarding anything He may be telling them.

## ASSIGN CHAPTERS FOR THE NEXT SESSION

Prior to session 1, group members should read chapters 1 and 2 of *The God I Never Knew.* Then, as you wrap up each session, remind participants of the book chapters to be read before the next meeting.

## SESSION 1    AM I MISSING SOMETHING?
## (CHAPTERS 1 AND 2)

### Introduction

While many believers have made the wonderful discovery of the Holy Spirit's ministry in their lives, too many other Christians virtually hold the third member of the Trinity at arm's length—from fear, confusion, or misinformation of who the Holy Spirit is and of the personal friendship, power, and guidance He offers everyone who believes in Jesus Christ.

Unfortunately, such hesitancy only prevents believers from thriving in their faith. In fact, Jesus considered the Holy Spirit's ministry so crucial that, on the evening prior to His crucifixion, He told His disciples, "And I will pray the Father, and He will give you another Helper, that He may abide with you forever—the Spirit of truth, whom the world cannot receive, because it neither sees Him nor knows Him; but you know Him, for He dwells with you and will be in you" (John 14:16–17).

Jesus knew that once He ascended to heaven, He would no longer be physically available on earth to help and instruct His followers. But God had a magnificent long-term plan in place: to give us the Holy Spirit ("another Helper") to indwell and abide with all believers—empowering, teaching, and guiding us to live God's way in a hostile world.

In this study we're going to explore who the Holy Spirit is, His ministry in the hearts and lives of God's people, and His role in helping us live the joyful, successful Christian life.

### Reflection and Discussion

1.  Do you identify with the author's experience of not really knowing much about the Holy Spirit earlier in his Christian journey? In the early days of your faith, what was your understanding of the Holy Spirit's identity and role in the Christian's life?

2.  As Robert was departing for Bible college, his pastor advised him, "Watch out for people who talk about the Holy Spirit." What do you suppose was behind this pastor's warning? Have you ever felt this cautionary about the Holy Spirit? Why?

3. Robert writes, "Most Christians hold a distorted, inaccurate, or incomplete view of the third member of the Trinity.... Too many have resigned themselves to perpetual defeat in their battles with temptation or to stumbling through life making decisions with nothing more than their own flawed reason to guide them. Others live a dull, powerless brand of Christianity." Do you agree or disagree with Robert's assessment of most Christians? Explain your thoughts. If indeed many or most believers are not as strong, loving, joyful, or effective as they can be, to what would you attribute their weakness?

4. Jesus promised His followers "the Helper, the Holy Spirit, whom the Father will send in My name" (John 14:26). Think back on your own Christian walk: how has the Holy Spirit helped you along the way? Share a recent example.

5. Jesus goes on to say, "He [the Holy Spirit] will teach you all things, and bring to your remembrance all things that I said to you." What does this passage mean to you personally regarding the Spirit's ministry in the Christian's life?

6. Robert writes, "Hearing God's voice begins by recognizing which member of the Trinity is tasked with speaking to us in this season of history. It is, of course, the Holy Spirit. The Father is on His throne. Jesus has been seated at His right hand and, according to Hebrews 10:12–13, will remain there 'waiting till His enemies are made His footstool.' The Holy Spirit, however, is active and present and commissioned to interact with us on the earth today." What are some ways in which a Christian might hear the voice of God? In such instances, who is doing the speaking? Can the Holy Spirit's guidance ever be contrary to God's Word or God's will? Why or why not?

*Key Verse*

Between now and session 2, claim Jesus's promise as your own: "These things I have spoken to you while being present with you. But the Helper, the Holy Spirit, whom the Father will send in My name, He will teach you all

things, and bring to your remembrance all things that I said to you"
(John 14:25–26).

### Prayer

Take time to share needs and requests for closing prayer. Be sure, too, to
thank God for providing His Holy Spirit to help, teach, guide, and empower
His children.

### For Next Time

To prepare for the next study and discussion, read chapters 3 and 4 of *The
God I Never Knew*.

## Session 2   Who Is the Holy Spirit?
## (Chapters 3 and 4)

### Introduction

If you're like many Christians, you may have encountered—even embraced—
some negative stereotypes regarding the Holy Spirit and the "Spirit-filled life."
The author of *The God I Never Knew* sure did. It took Robert a while, but
once he finally opened his mind and heart to the Bible's truth about the Holy
Spirit, he quickly realized the incredible benefits he had been missing!

In session 2 we will continue our look at who the Holy Spirit is. Notice
the emphasis on who, not what, for the Spirit is indeed a person and not some
vague cosmic force. In chapters 3 and 4, Robert clarifies from God's Word
that the Holy Spirit is God, just as God is God and Jesus is God. The Spirit
is God's glorious way of being a very present and active friend in the life of
everyone who trusts Christ as Savior and Lord.

We saw in session 1 that God sent the Holy Spirit to be our helper.
Today's study builds on the identity of the Spirit by showing that He is also
our friend...and that He is God.

### Reflection and Discussion

1. The author writes, "These stereotypes are indeed alive and
   thriving today among huge numbers of Jesus-loving people.

Many are sincerely reluctant to embrace the opportunity of a life-transforming relationship with the Holy Spirit because of such stereotypes." Robert contends that Satan is the author of the world's "weird" stereotypes of Spirit-controlled living. Why do you suppose Satan would not want God's people to embrace the help, friendship, and godhood of the Holy Spirit?

2. From your own observation and experience, what are some of the tactics Satan uses to convince us that embracing the Spirit's personal ministry might make us uncomfortable or weird? Have you struggled with such fears? Share your story.

3. In chapter 3, Robert cites four amazing benefits that the Holy Spirit brings into the life of the believer. Which one of these benefits stands out as particularly meaningful to you today? Why is this benefit significant to you? When the Holy Spirit is truly in control of your thoughts and actions, what kind of difference would this particular blessing make in your life?

4. Summarize the author's teaching of how the Holy Spirit speaks to us. If we, as Christians, do not believe we're hearing the voice of the Holy Spirit, what might be impeding such communication?

5. Robert writes, "The witness of Scripture is that the Holy Spirit is a full and equal member of the Trinity. The Holy Spirit is not a force, a thing, or an it. The Holy Spirit is God in one of His three persons. Treating Him as some sort of heavenly afterthought or a lower order of supernatural being we can choose to ignore is grievous." Look up and read aloud Matthew 28:19, John 14:16 and 15:26, and Acts 5:3–4. After each passage, address this question: what does this passage affirm about the person of the Holy Spirit?

6. Focus for a few moments on the final paragraph of chapter 4: "I encourage you to realize three truths before we go further on this journey: (1) the Holy Spirit was sent to be your helper, (2) He wants to be your intimate friend, and (3) the truth that makes those two statements most amazing of all is *He is God*." What do these truths mean to you personally, today? How would you assess the state of your present relationship with the Holy Spirit?

*Key Verse*

Between now and session 3, focus on this admonition from the apostle Paul: "Live by the Spirit, and you will not gratify the desires of the sinful nature" (Galatians 5:16, NIV).

*Prayer*

Take time to share needs and requests for closing prayer. Be sure, too, to thank God for providing His Holy Spirit as your personal helper and friend.

*For Next Time*

To prepare for the next study and discussion, read chapters 5, 6, and 7 of *The God I Never Knew*.

## SESSION 3    WHAT IS THIS PERSON LIKE? (CHAPTERS 5, 6, AND 7)

*Introduction*

"The Christian life is an upward journey," the author writes in chapter 7. "The moment we're born again, we are made *righteous*—put in right standing with God. But *sanctification*—becoming pure and more Christlike in our behavior—is a process. The Holy Spirit wants to be our partner and friend in that process."

In chapters 5, 6, and 7, Robert expands on the fact that the Holy Spirit is not an impersonal entity, but He is a person—with personality and a soul consisting of mind, will, and emotions. Knowing this assures us that God the Holy Spirit is a friend we truly want to know intimately, a helper we can trust absolutely, and a comforter we can lean on in times of distress. What an honor and privilege it is to have God living within us!

*Reflection and Discussion*

1. Numerous places in the Bible describe or demonstrate God to be *omniscient* (all knowing), *omnipotent* (all powerful), and *omnipres-*

*ent* (simultaneously everywhere). What does this tell you about the knowledge, strength, and presence of God the Holy Spirit? Why is this significant to you as a child of God?

2. Look up and read aloud Ephesians 3:20. What (or, more correctly, *Who*) is "the power that works in us"? How does it feel to know that your personal helper and friend is omnipotent? Are you taking full advantage of His power within you?

3. Robert writes, "The amazing news is that you have the Holy Spirit living within you, and as God, He has that same level of wisdom and knowledge [as God]. The Holy Spirit knows everything about everything, and He has committed Himself to be your teacher. He promises to lead you into all truth." What does the above paragraph help you appreciate about the mind of the Holy Spirit? Think of some specific ways in which He leads believers "into all truth."

4. In your own words, explain the basic differences between God's *general will* and God's *specific will*. What is the best way for us to learn and know God's general will? How are we most likely to learn and know His specific will?

5. Did it surprise you to read that the Holy Spirit has emotions— that we can cause Him grief or pain? What does this mean to your friendship with Him?

6. Look up and read aloud Ephesians 4:25–32. Robert writes, "Notice some of the specific behaviors that cause the Spirit to grieve: lying, sin, stealing, neglecting to give to others.... Because the Holy Spirit lives in every believer, mistreating any one of them involves mistreating the Holy Spirit in them." When you grieve the Holy Spirit, what happens to your intimacy with Him? Why? What do you need to do in order to restore intimacy with Him?

7. The author writes, "[A speaker asserted that] when the Holy Spirit warns us about something and we ignore His warning, it's the equivalent of 'stiff-arming' Him. In essence, we tell the Holy Spirit, 'I don't want You in my life. I don't want to listen

to You. I don't want to follow You—even though You only have my best interests in mind.' The speaker then described how we can't stiff-arm the Holy Spirit about sin one moment and then expect Him to speak to us about another matter a few moments later." Can you think of a time when the Holy Spirit was speaking to you and you "stiff-armed" His loving guidance? As you look back on the experience, do you think your action (or lack thereof) grieved the Holy Spirit? How did the situation turn out when you followed your own way instead of His? Is there an area of your life in which you're still clinging to your own way? What is God's Spirit telling you to do about it?

### Key Verse

"The fruit of the Spirit is love, joy, peace, longsuffering, kindness, goodness, faithfulness, gentleness, self-control" (Galatians 5:22–23).

### Prayer

Take time to share needs and requests for closing prayer. Then let the group know that at the start of prayer time, there will be a few minutes of silence to allow participants to engage in private prayer to deal with anything the Spirit may be telling them.

### For Next Time

To prepare for the next study and discussion, read chapters 8 and 9 of *The God I Never Knew*.

### SESSION 4   THE GRAND ENTRY (CHAPTERS 8 AND 9)

### Introduction

Just before He ascended to heaven, Jesus instructed His disciples that they were to wait in Jerusalem for "the Promise of the Father, 'which you have heard from Me.'" What was this Promise? "You shall be baptized with the Holy Spirit not many days from now" (Acts 1:4–5).

So wait they did, in faith, and history records that the Promise was fulfilled on the Day of Pentecost. The Holy Spirit descended upon 120 of Christ's closest followers like a gale-force wind. Eyewitnesses saw what they described as "tongues, as of fire" as God the Holy Spirit entered the lives and hearts of these early Christians. The Spirit empowered them to boldly proclaim the good news of Jesus Christ, and even in foreign languages so that Jerusalem's international visitors would understand and embrace the world-changing message. The Bible says that more than three thousand people believed in Jesus Christ that day alone.

But that was then and this is now, right? How does today's Christian receive the Holy Spirit along with His help and friendship and power for living? This session, based on chapters 8 and 9 of *The God I Never Knew*, explores the exciting truth that the Pentecost experience of being "baptized with the Holy Spirit" wasn't just a one-day event in history; it is for *every* believer, here and now.

### Reflection and Discussion

1. In light of the author's description of Jerusalem during the celebration of Passover and Pentecost, in what ways were the timing and manifestations of the Holy Spirit's entrance strategic to the spread of Christianity?

2. According to the author, "On Pentecost Sunday, the outpouring of the Holy Spirit changed everything." What were some of the most startling changes that took place? Why were these changes significant—then and now?

3. Romans 8:1 tells us, "There is therefore now no condemnation to those who are in Christ Jesus, who do not walk according to the flesh, but according to the Spirit." What does walking "according to the Spirit" look like to you? What difference does (or should) His presence make in the daily life of the believer?

4. After being filled with the Holy Spirit, Peter preaches to the crowds.

Look up and read aloud Acts 2:38–39. What is the gift Peter tells the people they will receive if they believe in Jesus Christ? Was this promise meant only for those to whom Peter was preaching on that day? If not, to whom, and for how long, is the promise valid?

5. Based on chapter 9 of *The God I Never Knew,* how would you respond to someone who contends that "Pentecost was a one-time event in history. It's not for Christians today"?

6. Robert recalls placing conditions on his desire to receive the fullness of the Holy Spirit, wanting to do so only on his own terms. Why do you suppose he didn't see much change in his life as a result? What should be the attitude of someone who wants to receive this gift of God?

7. When he finally caught on that we receive the Holy Spirit's fullness wholeheartedly, by faith, Robert prayed, "God, I trust You and I want everything You have for me. I want to be the most effective servant of Yours I can possibly be. I want to be empowered the same way the disciples were in the upper room. I want Your gifts. I want Your empowerment. I want You, Holy Spirit of God." What differences are apparent to you between his initial prayer and this one? Why do you suppose God honored *this* prayer and helped Robert appropriate the full presence and power of the Holy Spirit in his life?

## Key Verse

"Repent, and let every one of you be baptized in the name of Jesus Christ for the remission of sins; and you shall receive the gift of the Holy Spirit. *For the promise is to you and to your children, and to all who are afar off, as many as the Lord our God will call*" (Acts 2:38–39).

## Prayer

Take time to share needs and requests for closing prayer. Let the group know that you will begin prayer time with a few minutes of silent prayer for participants to talk personally with God.

## For Next Time

In preparation for the next session's reflection and discussion, read chapters 10, 11, and 12 of *The God I Never Knew.*

## SESSION 5   THE POWER TRANSFER
## (CHAPTERS 10, 11, AND 12)

### Introduction

Most modern-day Christians are aware of the biblical doctrine of water baptism. After a person receives Christ as Savior, being baptized with water is an act of obedience to God's Word that symbolizes the death and burial of our former, sin-centered life and our appropriation of new life in Jesus Christ.

But what many well-intentioned believers do not realize, and may not have been taught in their churches, is that there are actually three baptisms for the Christian—not just one. These three baptisms can be embraced with joyful enthusiasm because they bolster the believer with new life, comfort, power, and guidance from our Creator God Himself, through the personal ministry of the Holy Spirit.

In this session we will examine the three baptisms, with special focus on the third. Many Christians, including some famous and revered leaders of the faith, were not fully aware of this third baptism until later in their Christian walk—and their lives were never the same once they embraced it.

Does God have a similar discovery in store for you?

### Reflection and Discussion

1. In your own words, highlight the key differences between the three distinct baptisms detailed by the author: (1) baptism *of* the Holy Spirit, (2) water baptism, and (3) baptism *in* (or *with*) the Holy Spirit. In each case, who does the baptizing? What is signified by each baptism—and what is the end result?

2. At the start of chapter 11, Robert tells the story of the great evangelist D. L. Moody, who for years of Christian ministry felt

he had "received all the Holy Spirit there was to get" when he was saved. But years later, Moody experienced a life-changing, ministry-empowering baptism in the Holy Spirit. What was your reaction as you read this story?

3. Look up and read aloud Acts 8:12–16. What does this passage tell us about the need for every believer to receive baptism in the Holy Spirit?

4. Regarding Acts 8:12–16, Robert observes, "Notice what this passage *doesn't* say. It doesn't tell us that when the apostles in Jerusalem heard that Samaria had received the Word of God, they sent Peter and John who gave them the right hand of Christian fellowship *because they had everything they needed.* In the early years of my Christian walk, this is precisely what I was taught. I was told that once I was saved and water baptized, I had everything I needed to live the Christian life. Of course, now I know that without receiving the Holy Spirit, I was living a powerless and defeated life of minimal effectiveness in God's kingdom." Has your previous instruction or experience with baptism been similar to that of the believers in Acts 8, D. L. Moody, and Robert? Why do you suppose so many Christians are not aware of (or are skeptical, or even frightened by) the "third baptism"—baptism in the Holy Spirit?

5. Robert writes, "Moody later said that he was never the same after the day he was baptized in the Holy Spirit. He realized that almost everything he had accomplished in ministry prior to that moment had been done in the power of his own limited flesh. Afterward, he saw tens of thousands saved in revivals everywhere he went." We may not be called to evangelistic ministry as was D. L. Moody, but what benefits do God's people miss out on if pride, fear, controversy, or confusion prevents them from opening their hearts to the fullness of the Holy Spirit? Be as specific as you can.

6. In chapter 12 Robert observes, "Note that to turn Sarai into Sarah, God had to first take out the *i.* We can learn a lot of truth in that

little detail. Receiving the baptism in the Holy Spirit requires humility and selflessness. Prideful and self-centered people simply don't yield themselves to the baptism in the Holy Spirit." From your reading of *The God I Never Knew* and God's Word, describe the heart and mind of someone who is not open to receiving the "third baptism." What, in your opinion, holds him or her back from asking for this blessing? What heart qualities are essential prerequisites for receiving the fullness of the Holy Spirit?

7. Has God been speaking to you regarding your relationship with Him through His Spirit? What is He saying to you?

### Key Verse

"Therefore, leaving the discussion of *the elementary principles of Christ,* let us go on to perfection, *not laying again the foundation* of repentance from dead works and of faith toward God, *of the doctrine of baptisms,* of laying on of hands, of resurrection of the dead, and of eternal judgment" (Hebrews 6:1–2).

### Prayer

Take time to share needs and requests for closing prayer. Let the group know that you will begin prayer time with a few minutes of silent prayer for participants to talk with God personally about what He may be revealing to them.

### For Next Time

In preparation for the next session's reflection and discussion, read chapters 13, 14, 15, and 16 of *The God I Never Knew.*

### SESSION 6   THE GIVER
### (CHAPTERS 13, 14, 15, AND 16)

### Introduction

God's Word clearly teaches that the Holy Spirit bequeaths supernatural aptitudes and abilities, or "spiritual gifts," to Christians in order to edify one another and advance the kingdom of God. On that there is little debate. But over the years, and especially during the past century, contention has arisen regarding some of the specific spiritual gifts listed in God's Word. Many Christians believe that some of the spiritual gifts were provided only to help leverage the initial launch of Christianity, while many others believe that all of the gifts remain fully operational today.

The author of *The God I Never Knew* counted himself among the first group—until some of those "temporary" gifts were manifested in his own life. Now he believes wholeheartedly that "a loving and good God designed these gifts expressly for our benefit and blessing. What a tragedy that so many of God's children have rejected these gifts. Their rejection grieves the Holy Spirit and hinders the body of Christ."

Whatever your personal background, approach this session with an open mind and heart, and be loving and respectful with any participants who might disagree with you. The concepts presented here may affirm what you already believe, or they may help you gain greater understanding and appreciation for Christians whose beliefs are different from your own.

Regardless of your view on the subject, the triumphant message of these chapters is that "if you will open yourself up fully to the Holy Spirit, He will give you what you need, when you need it. Ask Him now to manifest His gifts through you 'as He wills' for the 'profit of all.'"

### Reflection and Discussion

1. When you hear the word *charismatic* in connection with the Christian faith, what comes to your mind? How does the author distinguish between cultural stereotypes and the biblical meaning of this term?

2. In the New Testament's original language, the term *charismata* means "grace gifts," particularly in reference to spiritual gifts given to believers by the Holy Spirit. In your own words, define *spiritual gift*. Are spiritual gifts exclusive to pastors, evangelists, and other Christian workers? What is the general purpose for which Christians are given such gifts?

3. Robert presents examples of what he calls discerning gifts of the

Spirit, which include a word of knowledge, discerning of spirits, and a word of wisdom. Briefly explain what each gift is, what it is *not,* and how its responsible use can benefit others in the body of Christ.

4. Can you imagine ways in which the above spiritual gifts might be used *irresponsibly* by an egocentric Christian? What negative consequences do you envision from such misuse?

5. In chapter 15, Robert discusses declarative gifts of the Spirit. These include messages of encouragement, messages in unknown languages (commonly referred to as tongues), and interpretation of unknown languages. In your own words, briefly explain each of these spiritual gifts and how its intended use can edify and benefit the body of Christ.

6. If you do not personally exercise the gift of speaking in unknown tongues, does the author's treatment of the subject in chapter 15 open your mind to the gift's viability for modern times? Why or why not? Would you be willing to take this particular manifestation of the Spirit before the Lord in prayer?

7. Chapter 16 explores what Robert calls dynamic gifts of the Spirit, including faith (supernatural confidence in God's promises and provision), healings, and miracles. Define each of these spiritual gifts. How might the Holy Spirit use each in your life to minister to others?

8. While 1 Corinthians 12 deals extensively with spiritual gifts, the apostle Paul follows this chapter with his famous discourse on what subject in 1 Corinthians 13? What important message do you think Paul is conveying regarding our use of spiritual gifts?

## *Key Verse*

"For to one is given the word of wisdom through the Spirit, to another the word of knowledge through the same Spirit, to another faith by the same Spirit, to another gifts of healings by the same Spirit, to another the working of miracles, to another prophecy, to another discerning of spirits, to another *different* kinds of tongues, to another the interpretation of tongues. But one and the same Spirit works all these things, distributing to each one individually as He wills" (1 Corinthians 12:8–11).

## Prayer

Take time to share needs and requests for closing prayer. Be sure to also pray that a spirit of love would trump any disagreements that may have surfaced during the discussion…and that God would clarify any confusion or doubts that may linger in the hearts of group members.

## For Next Time

In preparation for the next session's reflection and discussion, read chapters 17, 18, 19, and 20 of *The God I Never Knew.*

## SESSION 7    THE LANGUAGE OF FRIENDSHIP
## (CHAPTERS 17, 18, 19, AND 20)

## Introduction

There's no way around it: The spiritual gifts of speaking and praying in unknown languages have prompted fear, contention, and confusion among Christians for decades. Without a doubt, there are very loving, authentic, effective, Spirit-filled Christians on both sides of the issue, and 1 Corinthians 13–14 make clear that the last thing our Lord wants is for us to be judgmental or divided over these gifts.

Because the issue has created so much uncertainty and confusion among believers, Robert devotes four entire chapters to examining the topic. As you read these chapters, you'll have no doubt about Robert's viewpoint on these spiritual gifts. And while his views may or may not align with your own background and beliefs, we think you'll find that Robert has made every effort to present and support his perspective calmly, fairly, with love, and by "rightly dividing" the Scriptures with integrity.

As you process his presentation, ask the Holy Spirit to verify or clarify His truth and His will for you. Listen to His voice with a heart and mind open to whatever He may have in store.

## Reflection and Discussion

1. What was your reaction to Jack Hayford's story at the start of chapter 17? In your opinion, did the "well-known minister" respond the way Jesus would have responded? What would a more loving response look and sound like?

2. Robert writes, "I believe one of the great tragedies of the last one hundred years of church history has been the way Satan, the enemy of the church, has successfully made this particular gift so controversial and successfully made huge segments of the body of Christ reluctant to embrace *any* of the empowerments of the Holy Spirit. I know because I was one of them." If the author is right about Satan's role in this issue, why do you think Satan has engaged in such a strategy? Do you agree that the controversy has made many believers reluctant to embrace the ministry of the Holy Spirit at all? Have you, or people you know, been missing out on the fullness of the Spirit because this particular issue has been "off-putting"?

3. Explain the key differences between the *gift* of tongues and the *grace* of tongues. (To review, see chapter 17.)

4. Robert cautions how some believers have developed "a rigid obsession with 'the initial evidence of speaking in tongues' as being the only valid indicator of Holy Spirit baptism." Why is this emphasis a misinterpretation of the Bible's teaching? What do you think are some of the practical and spiritual dangers of this obsession?

5. Look up and read aloud 1 Corinthians 14:4–19. In your own words, summarize Paul's guidance regarding speaking and praying in tongues in public settings and private settings.

6. Paul writes in 1 Corinthians 14:4, "He who speaks in a tongue edifies himself, but he who prophesies edifies the church." What does the term *edify* mean to you? Is Paul saying, "Don't speak in tongues"? Describe the balance Paul is advocating.

7.  If you speak and/or pray in tongues, do you relate to the author's experience and counsel on how to receive this gift? Share your own experience. If you do not speak or pray in tongues, what was going through your mind and heart as you read the author's account along with his supporting scriptures? Are you open to this gift if God indeed has it in store for you?

8.  The author writes, "You can trust Him. As James tells us, 'Every good gift and every perfect gift is from above, and comes down from the Father of lights, with whom there is no variation or shadow of turning' (1:17). If there ever was a good and perfect gift that came down from the Father, the Holy Spirit is that gift. He is good. He is perfect." Is every spiritual gift a good and perfect gift from above? As you process the concepts presented in these chapters, what is the Lord telling you—about Himself, about His Spirit, and about your journey with Him?

### Key Verse

"Let all things be done for edification. If anyone speaks in a tongue, let there be two or at the most three, *each* in turn, and let one interpret. But if there is no interpreter, let him keep silent in church, and let him speak to himself and to God.... For God is not the author of confusion but of peace" (1 Corinthians 14:26–28, 33).

### Prayer

Take time to share needs and requests for closing prayer. Let the group know that you'll begin prayer time with several minutes of silent prayer. During this time, encourage participants to place any questions, confusion, or struggles regarding the content of this session before the Lord and to trust Him for answers.

### For Next Time

In preparation for the next session's reflection and discussion, read chapter 21 of *The God I Never Knew* and review key points you have noted in chapters 1–20.

## SESSION 8  YOUR NEW BEST FRIEND
## (CHAPTER 21)

### Introduction
God the Holy Spirit is available to all Christians. He thrives on being your helper and friend, a close companion who daily empowers and enables you to make better choices and honor God with your life. He wants to be your new best friend. All you need to do is ask, in faith, believing that God the Father and God the Son keep their promises.

- They do, and they will.
- What an incredible gift! Just ask, receive, unwrap, and enjoy.
- Your life will never be the same.

### Reflection and Discussion
1. After sharing the story of the poor man who sailed the Atlantic on an ocean liner and skipped meals because he didn't think he was entitled to them, Robert writes, "Jesus sent the Holy Spirit as a wonderful gift—a gift better than having Jesus Himself with us—and the price for His presence in our lives was fully purchased by Jesus on the cross. The Holy Spirit came with all the other amazing blessings of salvation. But some believers never receive and unwrap the gift. Instead, they live lives of cheese-and-crackers Christianity. They muddle through this world powerless and deprived of the richness of God's presence, consoling themselves with the knowledge that heaven awaits by and by." Do you personally know Christians who are living the way the author describes? Without naming names, what about their lives indicates to you that perhaps they have not received and unwrapped the incredible gift of the Holy Spirit's fullness?
2. Jesus says, "If you then, being evil, know how to give good gifts to your children, how much more will your heavenly Father give the Holy Spirit to those who ask Him!" (Luke 11:13). What do Jesus's words tell us about God's desire for every Christian to be filled with the Holy Spirit? According to this verse, how does one receive the Holy Spirit?

3. Robert affirms, "Experiencing His power and presence really is as simple as just asking and receiving. Our heavenly Father receives joy and pleasure when He gives the Holy Spirit to those who ask. Just as with the salvation experience, baptism in the Holy Spirit is a free gift from the Father that you can receive by faith." Why do you think appropriating such an important gift is not more complicated than merely asking and receiving? If you have not yet received baptism in the Holy Spirit, is there anything that would keep you from asking God and receiving this wonderful, free gift today?

4. In chapter 21, Robert reminds us of several of the benefits and blessings that friendship with the Holy Spirit brings. As you review that list, which of these are especially welcome in your life today? Why?

5. Looking back over the previous chapters of *The God I Never Knew,* what would you identify as your most meaningful "aha" discoveries about the person and ministry of the Holy Spirit? Why are they significant to you?

6. What has God been saying to you during this study? Is there an area of your life in which you've learned to trust Him more than before? As a result of reading the Scriptures and the book, has the Holy Spirit prompted you to take any new steps in your spiritual journey?

### Key Verse

"If you then, being evil, know how to give good gifts to your children, how much more will your heavenly Father give the Holy Spirit to those who ask Him!" (Luke 11:13).

### Prayer

Ask the group for needs and requests for closing prayer. Tell them that, as you've done in previous sessions, the first few minutes will be silent prayer so group members can talk privately with the Lord regarding their relationship with the Holy Spirit.

## *From Here On*

Now it's time to enjoy your relationship with your new best friend, God the Holy Spirit. He's there for you! Walk closely with Him, and take delight in His counsel.

# ACKNOWLEDGMENTS

I want to thank the following people:

- Debbie, my wonderful wife of thirty-one years, for being my best friend on earth and demonstrating these truths every day.
- The elders, staff, and members of Gateway Church, for receiving these truths with such joy and for walking in them.
- David Holland, for working with me through this project and helping me clearly express these truths.
- Judy Woodliff, my faithful assistant for nearly nine years, who encouraged me to put these truths in print and who is with the Lord now.

# About the Author

**ROBERT MORRIS** is the founding senior pastor of Gateway Church, a multicampus, evangelistic, Spirit-empowered church in the Dallas/Fort Worth Metroplex. Since it began in 2000, the church has grown to more than nineteen thousand active members.

He is featured on the weekly television program *The Blessed Life,* seen in approximately ninety million homes in the United States and in more than two hundred countries around the world.

Robert holds a doctor of letters from the King's University, which is given to those who have made substantial contributions to their respective fields through published works. He is the best-selling author of nine books, including *The Blessed Life, From Dream to Destiny,* and *The Power of Your Words.*

Robert and his wife, Debbie, have been married for thirty years and are blessed with one married daughter, two married sons, and two grandchildren. They reside in Southlake, Texas.